THE CONNECTION
PHENOMENON

MATTHIAS JACKEL

The Connection Phenomenon
First published in 2018
Copyright © 2018 Matthias Jackel

ISBN
Print: 978-0-6483403-0-0
Ebook: 978-0-6483403-1-7

All rights reserved. No part of this book may be reproduced, stored in a retrieval system, or transmitted by any means (electronic mechanical, photocopying, recording, or otherwise) without written permission from the author.

Because of the dynamic nature of the internet, any web addresses or links contained in this book may have changed since publication and may no longer be valid. The information in this book is based on the authors' experiences and opinions, the views expressed in this book are solely those of the author and do not necessarily reflect the views of the publisher, and the publisher hereby disclaims any responsibility for them.

The author of this book does not dispense any form of medical advice, legal, financial or technical advice either directly or indirectly. The intent of the author is only to offer information of general nature to help you in your quest for personal development and/or self-help, in the event you use any of the information in this book the author and the publisher assume no responsibility for your actions. If any form of expert assistance is required, the services of a competent professional should be sought.

Publishing information

Publishing, design and production facilitated
by Passionpreneur Publishing
www.PassionpreneurPublishing.com

Dedication

To my wonderful wife, Alexandra 'Akeesha' and my great kids, Jasmin, Julia, Anouk-Aimée and Louis, my amazing family and to my deep friends. You are my biggest inspirations and my ardent supporters, who help me to walk my way. I love you all.

Contents

Prelude 7

Chapter 1 (C) = 𝅗𝅥
    Losing Connection 17

Chapter 2 (C#) = 𝅗𝅥
    Feeling Connected 35

Chapter 3 (D) = 𝅗𝅥
    Business Connection 51

Chapter 4 (D#) = 𝅗𝅥
    Inner Connections 71

Chapter 5 (E) = 𝅗𝅥
    Brain Connections 87

Chapter 6 (F) = 𝅗𝅥
    Global Connections 103

Chapter 7 (F#) = 𝅗𝅥
    Daily Connections 115

Chapter 8 (G) =

Human Connections 129

Chapter 9 (G#) =

Balanced Connections 143

Chapter 10 (A) =

Connect Yourself 159

Chapter 11 (A#) =

Counter-Connections 183

Chapter 12 (B) =

A Connection Ambassador 201

Outlook (C) =

Fadeout: Final Words 213

Sources and Further Information 215

Testimonials 217

Acknowledgements 220

Prelude

For me, writing this book was a five-year process and many huge hurdles had to be overcome.

A good book is literally supposed to speak to you. But if I showed up right here, right now, as a speaker in front of you or your team, the first eight-ten minutes wouldn't even involve any speaking!

Instead, the first few minutes would provide a tangible experience. Rhythmic instruments would be provided to the audience and we'd get the music started in an interactive live act.

Most people would respond with surprise, especially the critics and sceptics among the lot. But eventually, everyone would be amazed and joyful, their experience taking them to a place that they never believed possible.

This is what happens even before the first "hello" is spoken.

What I do with my clients and audiences is always experience-based. In this book, unfortunately, it is impossible to have you make music with me.

So I'm writing about an experience you cannot experience yourself at this point in time.

I also had to wrap my head around what I experienced during all these events. Conclusions came to mind but there was a mismatch between what I saw in our projects and my own business and personal life. It took me years to understand that even the best conclusions mean nothing if they are not put into practice. Let me tell you how I resolved this issue.

Everyone has a story about their relationship with music. You may remember how you "learned" music. I personally feel that rehearsing the flute in pre-school classes damaged my brain. Playing the triangle in the school orchestra was quite stressful. And the teacher who presented the pandeiro as a tambourine was so boring because he had no clue how wonderful that instrument was. I also remember how the piano teacher damaged my soul when he shouted at me because of a wrong note.

Your early experiences with music lessons might not have been positive either. Music is one of the most intense explorations young people can make. It's up to the teacher to foster a curious mind for a wonderful world or create misleading mindsets by reducing music to a monotonous practice. Some are also guilty of telling students that they have no talent, are not musical or not rhythmical, all of which is nonsense.

Voltaire said, "Music, as it stands today, has been reduced to performing complex composition, but what becomes only complex won't please anyone in the long run."

And Issac Stern once said, "The greatest crime a musician can do is to play notes instead of making music."

I had not heard these statements when I was younger. So in my mind, music became synonymous with embarrassment, labour, effort, struggle and stress. And unless you are a professional musician with a spiritual attitude like Miles Davis, chances are you also feel the same way.

Now imagine that you come into a room and are faced with a challenge. Given your past, your mind insists that you are not a musician. And then, you sit down on the chair with a drum or some other rhythm instrument in your hands. You may think to yourself: "Why on earth do I have to do that?"

The fact that it turns into a major success anyway is because we're not trying to do what people used to do previously when it came to making music. We don't treat it as performance art.

The second, more important, reason why it succeeds is because of the positive vibe between the participants that gets injected into the group. It may not be conscious in the beginning but it slowly becomes apparent.

We don't name this new vibe right away as the impact of it would require some reflection, but this book is certainly intended to unfold further details about it later on. Initially, people are thrilled by the sheer fun and energy created. That is the wave we surf during the events.

But how come a serious-looking man approaches me backstage during a professional sales motivation kick-off event, asking if he can give me a hug? This is because the events create a sensation beyond mere entertainment. This is a feeling that makes the vast majority of them join into the drumming for the duration of 30 minutes or several days, depending on the length of the event. Eventually, they leave the room with some sort of change in their mindset.

Understanding the deeper reason for that changing mindset may become the start of a transformative process affecting both, you and your organization. People change. And this leads to change within the organizations or companies where they work.

But how can people possibly change?

There are actually three ways of learning. The first way is via rational thought, which is probably the most noble way. The second way involves copying others, which may be the easiest way. Lastly, you can also learn from experience.

People say that learning by experience hurts the most. But to me, it seems like the only effective way of learning. Because when you experience things, you have feelings. And your old emotions are unfolded too. This is the basis of any kind of lasting knowledge. And this is why we set our audiences to playing a rhythm instrument!

Over the course of the last few years, my teams have seen so many people perform together. And not a single event has ever failed!

As a result, I started thinking to myself that there must be a basic human desire that we serve i.e., the desire to be connected.

As a matter of fact, if I were to bring the whole book down to one line, then I would point out that we human beings want to feel connected. We are a social species and this makes us hardwired for connecting with others.

However, the way we've grown up—our culture and the economy around us—doesn't support that connectivity. Instead, it treats us as objects, rating us and comparing us with each other. Our worth lies in the way we look, our status, our know-how, our achievements and our possessions. We are all affected by this type of behaviour in our social lives as well as in business. No one is free from its effects, including myself. At the end, we are human beings conditioned by the way we grew up to become "human doings."

So when people come into our sessions, they experience something live that they are missing in their day-to-day lives. They can interact with other human beings without experiencing the usual barriers and judgements. They can contribute to the group as individuals and grow together.

But undergoing that experience doesn't mean that life becomes different the minute after. Old habits cannot be changed in 45 minutes; you need further reflection and practice to make this happen.

In 2004, I partnered with the worldwide Drum Cafe organization and opened the offices for Switzerland, Austria and Germany. Drum Cafe has become more of a movement than a "normal" company. It was started in Cape Town not long after Nelson Mandela became president of South Africa in 1994. This was a time of ambivalence and a period of joy, fear and hope during which many people anticipated bloodshed and war.

With 11 official languages, cultural differences and a minority which had held power for decades, South Africa needed to undergo a radical change. Under the guidance of President Mandela, bloodshed and war were averted and South Africa was transformed rapidly and profoundly into a "rainbow nation" which brought together cultures, races and communities under a unified banner.

The Drum Cafe took Madiba[1]'s philosophy as the core of its approach and during South Africa's time of transition, it brought the message of cohesion and unity to hundreds of companies across South Africa. The Drum Cafe facilitated communication and cooperation between black and white, male and female, old and young. It learnt to bridge the gap between the old and the new and to foster understanding and friendship between employees from vastly different cultural backgrounds.

---

1 In South Africa, "**Madiba**" is an affectionate nickname for President Nelson Mandela.

Today, Drum Cafe is running almost 300 events with 100,000 participants every month throughout the world. When Shakira was performing at the opening of the World Soccer Championship in South Africa, many drummers performing with her came from Drum Cafe. When South Africa was presented in the China Olympic games, the drummers on the field came from Drum Cafe. The concept even transformed to a production named *Drumstruck* that ran massively successful off-Broadway shows in New York as well as shows in Japan. At this point of time, *Drumstruck* still tours the world.

In 2014, I added my HR and people development experience to the services and founded andante communications GmbH (Ltd.) which was transformed into the Drum Cafe Academy in 2018, taking the experience of interactive Drum Cafe events to the next level, helping clients to understand why it works and what they can take out of it.

The core of the experience laid out in this book comes from personally having led close to a million people in drumming events. That became the university of my life. It became a massive empirical study about togetherness.

Now that we're talking about empiricism, there's a well-known problem in the empirical world called the problem of correlation. This means that if you try to find out the effect of something on a human being, you still have to deal with other effects layered over your study. Human beings don't stop living to become a part of a scientific study. They remain in their lives, so outside effects must be taken into account in the study.

For example, you might postulate that a kid playing the piano is developing a better brain compared to a kid that does not play the piano. The problem is that a kid that is growing up in a family that can provide piano lessons probably has more benefits available to him or her. This kid will have a lot more advantages compared to a kid that is growing up in a family where there is no time or money to fund piano lessons.

In actual fact, you never know exactly whether that piano-playing kid is "cleverer" because of the piano he or she learned, or because of all the additional family advantages that paved the way for an enhanced brain capacity.

In the case of drumming, the issue of correlation can be completely shelved because of the sheer number of people and the variety of clients that I worked with. These ranged from kids to adults, from people working in the factory belt to clerks, from administrative staff to mid-level and top-level managers, from CEOs to country leaders, from people in jail to celebrities and from joyful people to those hit by disasters. I have worked with people across all industries and across many cultures, ethnicities and countries.

There was no difference between them because they were all seeking the same thing. Those people were looking to get into contact with each other; they were seeking kindness and love.

This is what I do. From entertainment events and keynotes to workshops and trainings, I facilitate a development process by applying the Drum Cafe interactive concept and sharing my experience as well as existing world wisdom.

This book is meant to tell you the story of connectedness. It will also tell you how I lost that feeling of connectedness in my previous career. It will go into how connectedness happened in the last 14 years to the participants of our events and how it helped me reconnect. What does connectedness mean to businesses and the people working in it? How does our brain connect and how do you connect mindfully with people all around the world? How do you connect with other human beings, find balance and, finally, connect to yourself?

There are forces and reasons working against a more connected world, but you can overcome them and become a connection ambassador. This will benefit you and others.

Making music together offers incredible potential. It's an amazing way to discover yourself and life.

Of course, I'm excited to have you read the book and get inspired. As this is an individual endeavour, please don't expect a new leadership cookbook filled with management dogma. Instead, it is meant to provide you with thoughts and tools to start looking at what you *need* deeply inside instead of what you *want* superficially.

Human beings often want. For example, you *want* things to progress. But you *need* sleep. You never *want* sleep. But there is no progress without proper sleep. While we strive for the things we want, there are a lot of things that we're in need of to become complete and independent as individuals. You need to understand that principle on a greater scale. This is especially true today, when families, communities, businesses and the world are in need of leaders.

If this idea doesn't resonate with you and you stop reading this book, then at least consider one thing: seek what you desire. There is nothing wrong with any path, but it's important to remain connected with yourself and other human beings.

You can also visit *http://drumcafe.matthias-jackel.com* (and switch to English) to see how we can use music to connect people practically.

 "Music expresses that which cannot be said and on which it is impossible to be silent."

– Victor Hugo

Chapter 1 (C)
Losing Connection

Around the fifth month in the womb, your hearing system has developed quite a bit. You start hearing the constant beat of your mother's heart. And never again will you be as connected to anything or anybody in life.

In contrast to Western culture, Yoga, Buddhism, Daoism and Zen nurture the body as a central part of all experience and development. The body is the bridge to the now. To understand all the positivity that comes with that approach, just visualize a second prenatal experience back in the belly of your mother. Every movement that you made was within the confines of a physical and tangible border. You felt the walls of your mother's womb; when you reached out, you touched something. You tasted the amniotic fluid. Every experience that you went through was perceived in your brain as a bodily experience. But all you did was stay connected to your body.

And then, you were born. With the cutting of the

umbilical cord, you experienced your first unconscious yet dramatic separation while making your way into this world.

However, in the first couple of months, you still feel very connected to your parents and your surroundings, if everything goes normally. Nature makes sure that while you're so vulnerable, people around you take care of you, love you and pamper you.

For example, nature gives you big eyes compared to the size of your head. They capture attention and make people protect you. It gives you an angel's smile. The kind of a smile that a baby smiles after a couple of weeks touches you deeply while giving you endless sleepless nights. All my kids used to smile in that way.

Nature gives a baby these and many more advantages to make sure that, in the first months of life, it can literally do whatever it wants. We still treat the baby with unconditional love, because we're connected to its soul so intensively. When a little toddler starts crawling or walking on the ground, we would never shout, "You can do that better! I've seen other kids at the age of six or seven months and they crawl much faster than you, fool! So now get your f-ing butt moving!"

Except under pathological circumstances, it is impossible to imagine such behaviour.

After a while, when the ego comes in and we expect more from the kids, a disconnectedness develops and becomes wider and broader over time. We move away from connectedness and start expecting performance.

At this point, the child is expected to do something. Many families start judging their kids once the babies start speaking or walking upright. In fact, this judgment begins when the babies are supposed to start speaking or walking. "When did Peter, the son of our neighbours, start speaking his first words?" we ask ourselves. "And look at Mary over there. Gosh, she can already walk. Is everything fine at our end?" In this way, comparison begins right at the beginning of our lives.

Then you go to school. A classic school is an institution built to prepare a mass audience to behave well in an industrial economy, by using an educational system that has been developed in the last century. There is no doubt that if we restarted the school system from scratch, it would look different.

In actual fact, we have schools available where a set of specialists focuses purely on the potential of a human being, finding their one talent and nurturing it while managing their disabilities without focusing on them.

You find this kind of environment in special needs schools. But it would be interesting to see how this world would develop if every schoolkid enjoyed the same level of focus on his or her individuality.

Instead, we put kids in classes, create focus lessons, introduce marks, start at a time in the morning when most kids cannot perform well due to their biological clocks, judge their performance and compare and separate kids into different groups meant to follow different careers at an age when no one can possibly forecast what this person will develop into.

In addition to the physical disconnection comes the cultural disconnection, as a result of which we prioritize success, achievement and results over developing potential, humanity and wisdom. It's fair to say that I failed in the school system during my younger days.

I grew up in a family that was very open-minded and free-thinking. My father was a very successful musician. My mother was the unquestioned head of the home—straight-talking and emotional, but a human-sized heart of a person!

My dad was a famous jazz trumpet player, as a result of which I met a lot of great people and great musicians who were in and out of our house. My parents tell me that I once fell asleep, lying within the basedrum of the drumset, while the famous drummer Charlie Antolini was playing in a long-lasting jam session. At the age of nine or so, I even met Jerry Lewis backstage. At that time, I could perfectly imitate most of his sketches. But I just stood straight in front of him with my mouth shut until his body guard grunted, "Time's over." What a shame I couldn't speak English yet! Maybe even at that young age, I felt that I shouldn't move if I'm not good enough.

I started making music and, for some reason, I always compared myself to my father. My father was amazingly great and when he played with other upcoming musicians, he would make them fly on stage! His attitude and behaviour absolutely pushed these people to a level they had never reached before. When they played with him, they only had to push themselves one step further, and he made that possible.

But he was not the perfect person to work with when you were a beginner. He was a lovely person, but there was too much of a gap between what I could do as a musician and where he was musically. Giving me lessons or playing music together did not work out well.

He kept telling me the story of how he got into music and the amount of rehearsing he had done. If I wanted to go on stage and become a musician, then I had better rehearse a lot too. There is no way you can get into the public eye without knowing what you're doing. My father taught me this and I understood it perfectly.

Years later, I realised how destructive this way of thinking was for me. I realised that this is what we have done with music in our culture generally; we have emphasized excellence. If you want to make music, you need to be good! That's how most of the public looks at music.

People believe that you have to learn music and do it properly if you want to be allowed to go live and play along with other musicians.

This is actually quite a bizarre thing when you think about it.

We love drawing and painting and it would be absurd not to draw and paint just because there was a Picasso or a Van Gogh out there. Or think about soccer (football in other areas of the world). Just recently, many people switched on the TV and enjoyed watching famous teams with great soccer players in the 2018 World Championship. But naturally, when the game is over, people still go out on the streets and play soccer just for fun.

No one would ever avoid playing soccer just because there is a soccer star named Messi. People just play it.

But this is not the case with music. People believe that music is made for achieving excellence and not just for fun.

But when music was created thousands of years ago, it was not for the sake of endless rehearsal and the development of excellence. When prehistoric people came home from hunting and gathering and sat around a fire, they didn't assign an individual to present a musical performance. They didn't grunt, "Hey you! Get those two stones over there and entertain me! Make me happy!"

That concept of consuming and "please make me happy because my day was so bad" is something we developed only recently. It's an act of compensation. I come home and I want my surroundings to distract me from bad thoughts and improve my mood. I switch the TV on to save my day.

In those early days, it worked completely differently. Those people gathered around the fire and made music *together* to connect and feel each other, to see who actually survived the day. That's what music is for. And that's what we should be doing too.

I wasn't aware of that idea when I was young. I would have been happy if I had understood it earlier, because it would have completely changed the way I approached making music. Instead, I took up the challenge to become good in music. But no matter how good I became, I was always compared to my father. Being a teenager who wants to make his own way, it was not motivating to get on stage and be introduced as the son of Conny Jackel.

I was not old enough or established enough to stand that, so I made a decision not to pursue music as a profession. But I was still struggling with school for the reasons mentioned before.

My parents were kind enough to do a little bit of intelligence testing with me, and it turned out that I had a fairly high score. So my lack of success was not due to a lack of intelligence. Instead, I wasn't able to succeed at school because I was struggling with myself. I couldn't figure out what I was supposed to do.

So I stopped going to school and started an apprenticeship. I learned about electric installations such as bulbs and switches in people's houses. I did that for three years and, in hindsight, it gave me a lot of experience in the way people cooperate in a service-oriented business. It also made me understand that learning is meant to be applied to real life. I understood that mathematics is not just theoretical but can be used practically. Also, it gave me a bit of a timeout when it came to music.

I went back to school after my apprenticeship and started what should have become a rather successful management career.

I graduated from a professional high school, then started studying electronic engineering and data processing. I joined a company as a working student doing basic research for GUI (graphic user interface) software development.

I moved to the United States, worked with SUN Microsystems to understand their new X Windows library and returned to Germany to develop the new version of the GUI of our computer-aided design software–CALAY Systems. I'll never forget those creative early days of my career.

Then my company was sold to Siemens, as a result of which I came into contact with the culture and processes of a large (and, in those early days, typically German) worldwide corporation. I became a confirmed project manager; later on, I helped others develop the skills for project management.

I moved away from Siemens to become a software manager at the US company ScanData, specializing in high-speed scanning and the processing of paper-based receipts. The next step was moving to EDS to become the manager of an IT infrastructure support team. After that, I moved forward to Aspect Communications where I took on the role of application consulting manager. Aspect Communications was a US company making high-end call centre telecommunications hardware and software. I was running the team of application programming specialists who helped companies configure the software to their call centre business.

While running that team of consulting specialists, I also built up a training centre providing customized and open courses to our clients. We started with €50,000 in training revenue and increased business by 1,000% over the course of just two years.

After those early days in software development, which truly was a passion of mine, I became what is often called a job-hopper. While gaining so much experience in different industries and management roles, I finally realised that what I actually liked most was not doing the tasks itself, but getting the right people together in a team to do the tasks.

Whenever I took over a new role and set up teams and projects, I literally made myself redundant. It made me come to the conclusion that, instead of running teams and operations myself, I had to look for a role that would incorporate my nature. This idea led into a job with the consulting firm, Perot Systems, where I became the people development manager for Europe.

My job was primarily to recruit people for the various projects we had.

This was my career trajectory, in the course of which I gained a lot of knowledge. I'm glad to have gained so much work experience because it gave me a lot of insight into business and management, which is an important part of my personal portfolio. But the reason I tell you all this is a different one because my initial business experience also led me into running Drum Cafe and everything else that I'm going to tell you in this book.

I was earning quite a lot of money. During that business career, I also got married and had two beautiful children. Whenever someone asked me about my life, I responded that it was brilliant—look at what I've achieved, look at what management position I've climbed up to.

There I was, at 28, wearing a suit with a gold watch that I had just bought. I had a BMW that actually looked far too big for me. If I look back at pictures of those days, it makes me laugh. I was not myself. I was the perfect incarnation of a "successful manager."

But I was also frequently ill. I had severe back problems every now and then, and I was not really into my family.

I was successful because I had turned into an opportunistic performer. But I was absolutely disconnected.

And I didn't know it. If someone had asked me if

everything was all right, I would have argued any concerns away. The illness that I had, the back problems that appeared, the private challenges that came up, well, that's the way it is, that's the way it works. So I tricked myself, and I set achievement over being.

I lost my connection to my inner wisdom and the people around me, but I was very successful in the material world.

It is now important to me to be able to point out that I was not able to recognize how unhealthy the situation was. The hamster wheel truly looks like a job ladder when you look at it from the inside. And given how busy I was, I would have been in there forever.

The change had to come from the outside. And it occurred when my first wife separated from me in 2002.

Remember how we learn best? By experience!

Thinking might be the most noble path towards learning, but it requires a great deal of practice. And even then, thinking does not necessarily lead you straight into subconscious issues. Even if you get to that point with thinking, it requires a lot of courage to put any changes into practice.

Given that thinking is difficult to put into practice, most real change comes from outside pressure, instead of inside awareness. It seems as though this whole planet needs to be attacked by aliens before it recognizes how amazingly ridiculous our childish fights are!

When I got my wake-up call, everything I took for granted was now in question.

I had to rethink. Driven by the implications of a separation, I was open enough to reconsider music and what I could do with it. Could I play music to enjoy myself, calm myself and get back into balance? Or would I continue *not* to make music because I thought I was not good enough? I decided on the former and started making music. I built my first small audio studio where I could record music.

This was the turnaround that helped me to reincorporate music into my life. It led me into creating a novel version of recruiting, using music. It led me to become a partner at Drum Cafe, to found the Drum Cafe Academy and to earn my living with a business that allowed me to make music with hundreds of thousands of strangers.

In the 16 years since those days of unexpected change, I can count the number of times I have been ill with the fingers of just one hand! And I can count the number of times I had problems with my back with even less than that.

The experiences of one person may not be enough to conclude that there's a causal connection between the way you run your life and your state of health. But it made me think about the bonds of the early days and understand how they get eroded with success and possessions. And it made me realise that possessions always possess you. We can't connect with possessions, only with human beings.

Take the example of the house that you live in. Many people in the world buy a house to live in and then they think, "Well, I've invested so much money. This is it. I love my house. I want to be here." But if that house starts to possess you and makes you feel like you're never going to move out until you die, then it might become a golden cage one day. It might get to the point where you would rather separate from your partner and save the house instead of keeping your partner and getting rid of your house for a better quality of life.

It's the same thing with success. The more successful you are, the more you have to lose.

Freeing your mind is difficult if the mind is bonded to objects and status.

The one thing that I want to make you understand is the possible loss of connection while seeking success. We, as human beings, are hardwired for togetherness; that is what we're born for. But the culture we live in nowadays is built to disconnect.

We need to take into consideration that the ego and cultural conditioning work against connectedness. There is a great opportunity in recognizing the meaning of music and reshaping our relationship to music. It can help us experience connectedness, making us aware and helping us reconnect with people.

Barenboim once said, "In many ways, music is the best school for life, really. And yet, at the same time, it is a perfect means of escape from the world."

To him, the duality of music makes it a paradox. To me, it's only logical because to really understand life, you need to look at it from a distance, not from inside.

It helps to understand that by making music together, we feel connected and escape normal day-to-day activities. Plus, we also have a great way to understand what is happening between us.

You may say, "But that's the way the world works. We just have to deliver. There's no reward for being kind to each other and group-thinking. We are judged individually, so we have to perform."

It's true that the world used to be that way, and it still may be true. But the world is also changing.

One amazing gift that I received from attending thousands of corporate events is that I got to listen to so many famous speakers. And there was a commonality between their speeches about what is happening in this world. The world is undergoing massive change. People talk about globalisation, digitisation, the internet of things, automation, industry 4.0 and the volatile, uncertain, complex and ambiguous (VUCA) world nowadays. That world is here. And it's getting more demanding.

Some critics say that change was always happening, maybe on an even bigger scale than today. Take Germany as an example. If someone was born in 1900 and lived a long lifespan, then this person experienced several changes in political systems as Germany went from being an empire to a republic to a dictatorship and finally, to a democracy, while undergoing two truly disruptive world wars.

The monetary system changed six times, starting with the Mark and ending with the Euro. I don't even want to start with all the massive technological achievements in transport, industry, communication and media as the list would become too long.

So what's the difference between the last century and this one? The earlier change was massive but extremely concrete and coherent. People were all in the same boat, facing changes of global magnitude together.

Today, we are faced with diverse challenges at all levels, an occurrence which is changing our businesses and personal lives at a speed and a level that never existed before. With all the freedom and choice of today's changing systems come a completely new level of responsibility and pressure on the individual. The things that worked in the last century will not work in the future. The skills required to deal with the future are different from those we used in previous centuries. We need to open up our toolbox and acknowledge and appreciate what we have learned so far but also consider more.

The best way to experience, the best way to achieve and the best way to go through hard times is by doing it with other people whom you feel connected with. This sets the groundwork for the social intelligence required in the future.

Think about how connected you are today—to yourself, your body, your partner, your kids, your family, your friends, your neighbours, the community you live in and the world.

Listen carefully to your initial thoughts.

Don't limit your assessment to your professional links i.e., your colleagues, your team or the people you report to. These are important as well, but, at this time, it is more important to have a holistic view. Often, our focus is only on business connections. Once that becomes a strong area, it is likely that you will get out of balance in terms of connectedness to yourself and your social life.

You may think about whether you are taking ownership of your life and your responsibility to get that right.

You may assess your health by recalling the average frequency with which you pick up a cold, any back problems, headaches, blood pressure fluctuations or problems with being overweight. Your body always tells you a story. If these things are present, then there is a story behind them.

You may also apply these ideas of health assessment to the organization that you lead.

When I ask people to evaluate their level of

connectedness, I instantly hear them say, "But there are things that must be done alone. Connectedness is not everything. There are things that are only achievable if I separate myself and focus."

Yes, there are.

There is a nice African saying that provides a lot of guidance about what to do when: "If you want to go somewhere fast, you had better go alone and run. If you want to go far in life and complete a long-lasting journey, you had better go together with other people."

That is the balance that we all need to seek.

Sooner or later in this world, we are all told that we need to become successful. But what you need is to remain connected.

The rhythm of that heartbeat in the belly of your mum is the first thing that you heard in life. It is no wonder that a rhythm can reunite you.

It is no wonder that the rhythm of making music reunited me with myself. And it is no wonder I use the Drum Cafe rhythmic experience to help my clients transform from a company to a community.

Chapter 2 (C#)
Feeling Connected

Let me show you how it feels to connect people in just ten minutes.

Imagine that you're at a huge event venue with 2,000 seats. The client has booked Drum Cafe as the opening act of the day. The lights on the stage are on when the doors open. Two different banks have merged and the people of both stream into the hall, meeting as a group for the first time. They're expecting a presentation from the board leaders arguing in favor of bringing these two companies together for greater success.

But this expectation is not going to be fulfilled. Instead, they see percussionists on stage performing.

There are massive sounds and great grooves which lead into amazing stage entertainment.

When you look again, you see that each chair has a drum placed face down on it. It is a picture silently expressing massive power. You can be sure that the people coming through the doors know that once they all sit down, the room will fill up with pure energy.

We run a short percussion show while people take their seats. Once 80-90% of people are in their seats, four-three-two-one, we come to a complete stop. Of course, the performance was more than good enough for every audience to applaud.

With simple body language, we invite the audience to take the provided drum and turn that hand-clapping applause into a big rumble on the drum. Most of the people accept the invitation. Those who just watch the scene and do not join in right away are as welcome as those giving it a go and enjoying themselves.

Then we start organizing that rumble. We make it louder and softer, and we move it from left to right. People unconsciously realise that this is not only a fun piece, but also one that makes sense. It works in a healthy and childlike way which actually feels really good. Just getting it started and doing something agile means that you're communicating with each other because no one can join the rhythm without listening. Even that little left-right movement means you need to start communicating. You need to hear when the sound is supposed to get loud at the right time.

Then one-two-three-four. We count in the first Drum Cafe groove and only seconds later, 95% of the people are united in one common groove. Goosebumps spring up all over the place.

We stop the beat, pause for one bar, and restart. It may not work at the first attempt, which is taken with a friendly smile. But the second attempt always works because human beings are basically all seeking structure, so they fall into it. There is a change of absolute, dynamic power and energy when we come to a full stop in absolute silence and then restart again. Flowing back into high energy is a sensational feeling to the ears, the body and the eyes too, because you see people moving. By that point in time, people have already realised that they're performing together.

We have the left side continue drumming while the right side gets back into a rumble. Then the right side stops the rumble again, and we introduce a heartbeat—a boom-boom, boom-boom in sync with the neighbours on the left side of the room who are still playing the Drum Cafe groove. Then we flip sides. The left side is doing the heartbeat now, while the right side is playing the Drum Cafe opening groove again.

All that happens without a single word spoken.

After maybe eight or nine minutes, we ramp up the speed and close the circle by bringing it back to the mutual rumble of the start. After this first experience, everyone gets all loud and excited.

Ten minutes are over, and, if that is what the client is looking for, we can already stop here.

When people enter the room, they are sceptical about being able to work together. But this experience shows them that they can work together. In fact, they have done so already.

The question of the day, "Can you work as a team?" is not a question anymore. It has turned into reality. So there's not much more to say, except for, "Take that energy along and give your co-working a go tomorrow, in the same open-minded and agile way you did today. Then there's no question that you can make it together."

It's a simple but fundamental fact. When people return to their workplaces the next day, the world goes back to normal. Yet, it feels so much more complex and different because of the drumming.

Business and social structures have resulted in a mix of very useful and very unnecessary systems and procedures. You can truly question if these are required, since they seem to block cooperation between human beings. Still, when it comes to drumming, people continue to work together as before.

But there is also a deeper wisdom in the drumming.

To start digging into it, let's jump back in time to when I was the people development manager at Perot Systems. It was one evening after a classic recruiting event and we were thinking about how to improve our systems and procedures. We wanted to attract people as well as assess who would fit better into the organization.

I had developed assessment centres with the help of some external psychologists. These centres made people take a number of standard tests and evaluated their personalities and soft skills.

But the fact is that they never really worked properly. We were seeking unconventional people and using conventional measures such as standardized tests. What a pity.

We probably had one too many glasses of wine when I remembered the time when I was a drummer. A funny idea came into my mind—to view people as they joined into group drumming instead of doing the usual table exercises. We picked up the idea and went with it.

The next day, with our heads cleared, we worked out the specifics to make sure we could independently reaffirm any observations made during the drumming session.

We were seeking new project managers. So we hired a classic drum circle facilitator just to run a 45-minute session where approximately 15 candidates were given rhythm instruments and a short introduction before they drummed together. I had no experience with leading such a circle at that time and I also wanted to focus on observing.

The nature of a classic drum circle is to let the drumming flow. The facilitators have very little influence. It leads where it leads and self-experience is the centre of it all. That was perfect for us as we didn't want to entertain the candidates with drumming. Instead, we wanted to see what they made out of it.

The drumming was directly followed by a 30-minute introduction to the project management methodology applicable to our company. We asked the participants to imagine someone had heard their great performance and offered them a concert tour in the next 12 months to four major cities in Germany. They had another 45 minutes to structure the project from that day until they could perform at those four concerts, using the project management method shown before.

This method enabled us to observe group and individual performance in three ways within just two hours.

- We could observe people during the free drum circle session.
- We could observe people while they were being taught the project management methodology.
- We could observe them while they executed a short project management session live.

What we saw was absolutely astonishing, it was jaw-dropping.

The way people behaved while drumming was exactly the way they behaved in the exercise for project management.

You may have heard of the four phases of teambuilding, as theorized by Tuckman. Every team that is newly-formed goes through four steps of coming together. These are: forming i.e., coming together as a team, storming i.e., the positive, can-do spirit of every beginning, norming i.e., the introduction of rules and agreements to improve effectiveness and efficiency and performing i.e., developing into a constantly high-performing team. While every group goes through these four phases, it does so at different speeds.

In our experiment, the most interesting part was when, for example, individuals or groups resided relatively long in the storming phase of the drumming. During this time, they were just drumming, with little structure added to it. They were just enjoying the energy. If this happened, then they did exactly the same in the project management exercise. They would have long-lasting brainstorming sessions with little planning added to them. They would enjoy the excitement of pure action even though there was little improvement.

There were also those who skipped all the fun at the beginning and jumped right into norming. These were the people who went, "Hang on, wait a minute. I need to understand the drumming techniques first." They behaved similarly in the project planning, saying, "Not so fast. We need to set a project plan and define leadership roles first."

This happened so often that, after a while, we started making perfect predictions of team performance right after the drumming.

There was nothing wrong or right in the behaviour of the participants. Sometimes, a company needs "stormers," and sometimes, it needs "planners." Both are needed to form a vital team. The art lies in quickly finding out what tendency a person has.

We realised that, during drumming, people dropped any preconditioned roles and connected with their inner being. They showed us who they really were. They dropped any masks they had put on. They were no longer thinking, "I have to be like this or that" or "I have to behave in a certain way in order to get the job."

These masks are never to the benefit of the employee or the employer in the long run.

It was such an amazing experience to realise how we can get to know people better so easily that we decided to make it into a great people development program.

I haven't finished telling you the story of my employment career yet—the gap between those famous last days at Perot Systems and setting up Drum Cafe Germany.

September 11 happened and, a few months later, very much in sync with my separation, the changing economy had a major effect on my job. It changed from recruiting to outplacement as we had to lay off a number of people over the course of almost one year. This was another important experience that shaped my thinking.

When there was not much left for me to do but lay myself off, I decided not to pursue that route any further. Connecting to yourself sometimes means separating from what was and looking for some new pastures. I took the idea of drumming and music and put it together with what I had learned through my career and personal life to form a service which I planned to call "teaming and drumming".

I scanned the market and looked at what companies were out there, but there was literally no company at all in Germany which provided such a service on a professional level. However, I found Drum Cafe on the internet. It was an organisation that already had a history. It was famous throughout the world for doing interactive drumming shows at corporate events. We met in a café in London and became partners. For many years, I was rolling out the concept of Drum Cafe in Germany, Switzerland, Austria and many other places around the world.

The deeper wisdom in drumming was revealed to me over the years. Each time I repeated the shows, the effects reoccurred. Let me give you an example.

There is an exercise in our event called "big bangs." It's a combination of high-energy single strokes played on the drums. It can be indicated with fingers or by a dancer on stage. The audience responds to a certain number of strokes shown (say, three fingers up) with an equivalent number of bangs played with strong power on the drum.

When five fingers are shown, those five strokes are played and lead into a complete stop for at least one or two bars. We explain that holding that stop and experiencing the silence is a sensational feeling—a counterpart to the high-energy strokes.

One day, we had about 600 people drumming in an atrium and the sound was just massive. We practiced this one-two-three-four-five-stop element and, after a bit of rehearsal, everyone came to a perfect stop.

At that very moment, just by coincidence, there was a lady with high heels passing by on a stone floor. And everyone heard her loud and clear. She was walking click-clack, click-clack, click-clack.

It became very obvious that it was silence that helped the participants become conscious of that detail of the situation. No one would have heard the little sounds if they'd kept on performing.

A great interpretation of this phenomenon comes from the spiritual leader, the Dalai Lama: "When you talk, you are only repeating what you already know. But if you listen, you may learn something new."

For those who are more into science, there is another physical explanation available that is similarly impressive: the so-called Weber Fechner effect.

If you have a room full of 100 burning candles and you add one more candle to it, you probably won't notice the difference. But if the room is completely dark and you light up just one candle, it almost seems to explode in front of your eyes!

This is what silence means from a physical perspective. You need to calm your mind and stop your thinking if you want to notice that one candle that is going to light up somewhere near you. That one candle is a metaphor for the light of someone or something that you may or may not see, depending on the state of your consciousness. It is a question of distinguishing between *kronos*, the loudness of progress and *kairos*, the beauty and silence of the moment.

Such special moments made me curious.

But the real kick-off for making greater use of interactive drumming was a moment that was even more special. It was so amazingly special that it sounds a bit like a Hollywood movie plot. But it's a true story.

I was doing one of my classic Drum Cafe events. When I got off the stage, there was an area where we could meet with the people who attended the event. A lady approached me. Maybe she introduced herself, but I can't remember her name.

She asked me if I knew what I was doing there. I responded, "Of course, I know. We're doing an interactive drumming event."

"No, no, no," she said. "What you are doing here is actually a Shaman ritual."

At that point in time, I didn't know exactly what a Shaman ritual was. So I just stared at her.

She maintained a second of awkward silence, then looked straight into my eyes to say, "You know, you are using a very, very powerful tool. I just hope that you are a good person!"

This made me think about myself, what the drumming did for me and why every single event we did worked so perfectly.

That happened in 2012. Six years later, the number of interactive drumming sessions I had done added up to around 2,000 hours. Drumming had turned into a contemplative practice without me realising it. There is no other way I can explain how a cerebral and non-spiritual person like I used to be could have made it to where I am today.

I knew I wanted to change. But what I needed was

patience. This is what the years of running interactive drumming events helped me to develop. My mind became more conscious through an unconscious contemplative practice.

Today, I can summarize that the magic behind drumming is that thing called "connectedness." It is a vibe between participants in our events which is impossible to put across in words, sounds or videos. It is a sensational feeling only available to those who are physically in the room. When experienced often enough, it ignites the need to seek the feeling again. And it creates the willingness to actively recreate the feeling rather than waiting for the environment to provide it.

Only a few people seek extreme new experiences voluntarily. Most of us need to be pushed into it by an external force. The good news is that most people come to events to get news, to feel excited, to celebrate, to get motivated and to be entertained. These are the typical goals of events. There's also good food and a good party at the end.

But more than these superficial things, what people receive in our events is practice—they learn to practice appreciation and acknowledgement as well as silence and listening. They learn to focus on one thing while they also try something new. They recognise the sensation of being in a group and the power of a proper break. They learn to communicate clearly and focus on possibilities rather than failure. They feel connected.

Feeling connected means recognising and nurturing the link to yourself and others. It re-establishes the mind-body connection to help you understand and listen to your body once again. It is a deeper understanding between you and others and a way to access your subconscious mind. It activates your body and increases your vibration for a better life. It is about awareness and consciousness. Mindfulness starts when you experience the absence of mind.

This is where I pick up the Drum Cafe experience and provide a deeper understanding to our clients in the Academy projects and to you in this book.

Interlude

You may have come to this book because you experienced one of our services and want to go deeper into the topic.

In the chapters to come, I'm going to provide you with different views from various angles to help you understand. I will introduce you to exercises we did and tell you about the typical audience reactions. This will inspire you to gain access to your subconscious mind. I'll offer new and unexpected ways of experiencing your life in a group and on your own. I invite you to give it a try. I know it requires stepping out of your comfort zone and accepting the emotions that come up. Ideally, you will experience these in a group.

If you have no experience with our services yet, then you can still read on, since there is no information coming that requires any prerequisite knowledge. There are also many exercises coming that you can use on your own. However, if you are an event organizer, HR or NGO manager, leader of a team, the head of a company or principal of a school, this is a good time to mention that you can experience these effects live by visiting *http://drumcafe.matthias-jackel.com* (you can switch between German and English) and get an overview of the full list of our services. Nothing can compare to that.

Depending on your background, you might be sceptical about group dynamics and group exercises. You have a right to your opinion and your judgement. But did you ever wonder why so many people like to go to a stadium to watch a game? Or go to the cinema to watch a movie? Both are group experiences. No one would welcome watching the Super Bowl in a stadium just on their own. That wouldn't be fun, even if it is the best game ever.

Human beings just love experiencing life together. Of course, everyone needs balance. We sometimes seek solitude to get back on track. But the fact is that we would die without social contact on a deserted island. No one wants to live on a deserted island for very long. And social skills are best learned in a real group. Otherwise, it's all just theoretical.

You may also argue that you're required to deliver. Why should you waste energy with feelings? Well, a human being is a bundle of feelings. And if your feelings are not shown but hidden away, then it's not going to be good for you in the long run. Facing your feelings is what brings better results and outcomes. So, it is worth it to open up and gain awareness of your feelings. You need to get in touch with your feelings. Otherwise your feelings will turn into emotions and may cause the emotional reactions that are so hard to control and that you might often wonder where they come from.

The final question is: what happens if you love your comfort zone and you don't want to leave it? Well, it's true that humans are also lazy by nature. At this point, you may expect me to say that you have to bite the bullet and do it anyway. But you will see that that is not my style. I don't believe that things can develop nicely if there is a "must" or "should" behind them.

I prefer a playful approach and will provide you with ideas that will help you to find out and decide what resonates with you.

The bottom line is that the only way of increasing the playfield of life is by experiencing new things. Making music together is certainly one new experience. This book talks about what effect that has had on so many people in our events.

Chapter 3 (D)
Business Connection

What is the core of a corporation and how is it connected to musical performance?

There are a lot of theories out there explaining what makes a corporation tick. One attempt that I came across was outlined in a book called *Leading Radical (Radikal Führen,* available in German only) by Reinhold K. Sprenger whose excellent work I once had the pleasure of experiencing personally when we both did a one-day workshop for a Swiss company.

In the book, he raises the question of why people actually work together. His answer is basically that they do so because they want to solve a problem that they can't solve alone.

This results in the thesis that collaboration is the central value of a company. People work together if they have a problem that is linked to one of the following criteria:

- First of all, the problem should be important. In the most urgent cases, it is about survival.
- Next, the common problem is applicable to all of them. It touches all of them.
- Third, the problem is easy to understand and self-explanatory.
- Lastly, the problem cannot be solved alone.

These are the things that lead into people working together in a company. Or, as Mr. Sprenger quotes Ezra Pound with a twinkle in his eye, "Management is the art of creating problems that keep the crowd busy."

I had read this book out of curiosity when I prepared for that Swiss workshop and I thought about it all the way back to Germany. The interesting point to me is that, until now, we've had several hundreds of thousands of people making music together. For many of the people, it was a transformative experience or, at least, the first piece of the puzzle on the way to working together. But neither of the above four statements applied to the situation when they came together in music.

No one thought about the problem, nor was there any pressure or danger. It just happened. The participants certainly didn't consider the drumming to be important. And there was no common problem which was applicable to everyone at these events. As for Sprenger's idea that solving the problem should only be possible together, that also wasn't something that the people in the group were aware of, in the beginning. Most of the time, they were not eager to do the drumming, and they didn't think it was a good idea.

Nevertheless, it worked very well and became a great success.

Based on that, I believe that there's also a more natural way of working together, not driven by pressure but by the desire of the human being for a community that provides security, fosters potential and gives freedom for personal growth while working together towards a shared vision.

Without actually recognising it, the participants of our events enter a field where people are seen and respected and can develop together at the same time. It is a blueprint for a new work ethic.

I have broken this work ethic down into the three core qualities of a corporation and the three core qualities of people. All six of them can be observed live in our sessions. Let's start with the three business-related ones.

This is not meant to be the new dogma for leadership and running a business. Actually, my whole book is meant to get rid of dogmas and recognise the flexibility of the world. You need to see that there are many diverse ways in which you can become successful, however you choose to define success. You don't need a cookbook which tells you how to run your business or your life. You need structures and processes, means and tools to make things work. But you also need to be flexible.

Reacting in a flexible way to a new and changing situation is the first challenge created in our events.

People see the drums and straightaway, we get into a call-and-response dialogue. We play short and changing rhythm patterns and people respond to them. The word that best describes these responses is agility.

Agility has become a buzzword within a lot of companies. Agility can be experienced in the moment, when we get the drumming going. Agility is about getting things done. It's about moving forward. It can be applied to a group which starts performing the action and to those who ramp up the group's progress. Agility means you don't focus on failure. You don't think of the problem as a problem. You just get it going and then develop a solution while you're in the midst of things.

That's exactly what happens in those first eight or ten minutes of our sessions.

We start with very simple patterns for people to respond to. Then we ramp it up and make it more and more complex. Within a couple of minutes, people are playing grooves that they had never expected to be able to play upfront.

At one point, the complexity gets to such a point that it involves a combination of drumming, clapping and speed snapping that literally no one in the room believed he or she could do. But because they do it together, it sounds richer and wider and fuller than what I did on stage.

The thing is to remember that you have people around to do things together. And this is even more important to keep in mind when you're faced with a challenge that you consider too hard to achieve. In my example, most people thought the snapping was way too fast to do. But when they do it together, it actually sounds much better than they had expected.

The way it occurs causes people to laugh in relief. They laugh about something they were very sceptical about before. These are the four steps you undergo in the process of drumming:

- You face a new challenge.
- You think you can't do it.
- But you give it a go. You try it out, together with others.
- You realise that it's actually not that bad which gives you a feeling of merriment.

That, to me, is agility.

Collaboration lies at the core of the second quality to achieve a certain goal together.

The moment we see collaboration happen in our sessions is when we hand out the so-called boomwhacker instruments. The boomwhacker is a hard plastic tube that becomes a beautiful percussion instrument when taken in one hand and hit into the palm of the other.

The boomwhacker doesn't only provide a single percussion sound. The set we use consists of six different tubes, visually easy to recognize by size and colour and tuned into what is called the pentatonic scale. The pentatonic scale is an amazing subset of six out of the 12 tones of the full music scale that all our modern music is built upon. The beauty comes from the fact that even if all six boomwhacker tones are played at once, it creates a very pleasant harmony of sounds and no chaos.

We hand out one boomwhacker to each person and once people understand how to play it, we introduce a complex groove, starting with the group using the first C-tuned boomwhacker playing a very easy and steady beat.

Bang, two, three, four, bang, two, three, four, bang, two, three, four.

The second tube, the D, will also play an easy pattern that suits beat number one, leaving enough space for more to come. Patterns three, four, five and six will be added, one pattern for each tone of the pentatonic boomwhacker set. It is amazing to see how fast people internalise their groove and keep playing perfectly on their own.

People realise that they are playing something that no one in this room, not even a professional percussionist, could play on his own. This is because we have six different sounds and six different grooves playing at the same time.

As human beings, we have only four extremities. We have two hands and two feet to create a rhythm. We have our voices, which, if we are really trained, may give us the ability to sing a fifth rhythm while we are busy with our hands and feet. But when it comes to the sixth groove pattern, it is impossible for just one person to play them all.

In that moment, a very complex, syncopated polyrhythm is being played by this big group of drumming novices. It's also a very nice melody that is easy to remember, making it a long-lasting anchor for that special discovery. The insight is that there are things in life that we can only achieve together and not on our own.

When it gets really complex, we need to understand that we need others.

You can give that a try yourself at home. There is a nice exercise that I call the pineapple groove. It consists of two grooves that are played at once. One groove is clapped with your hand and one groove is spoken with your mouth. The groove to clap is a clave often used by huge groups in public.

It goes taa-taa-ti-ti-taa-ti-ti-ti-taa-ti-taa.

Most of us know that one from the sports events where thousands of people clap it. Just follow this link to listen to it if you like:

http://tcp-clave.matthias-jackel.com

The second part of the exercise is to say the word "pineapple" in a loop. This is because pineapple is a word made up of three syllables pronounced "pine-ap-pel" or "pahy-nap-ul."

Just follow this link to listen to this too, if you like.

http://tcp-pineapple.matthias-jackel.com

If you say "pineapple" in a loop and clap the stadium clave in parallel and same basic rhythm (i.e. at the same speed), then math will tell that you have three beats (or syllables) of pine-ap-pel over eight beats of the clave, making a groove pattern that repeats after only 24 beats.

http://tcp-pineapple-clave.matthias-jackel.com

I suggest dropping the book for a moment and trying to play those two patterns together, on your own.

You will realise quickly that it's going to take a hell of a lot of rehearsing to get it right.

But if you just do the clapping and have another person repeat "pineapple," then it is done within seconds.

So when a task gets complex, you need to get other people to participate in it. This way, you can spread complexity across the group and everyone is assigned a task that can be delivered without too much pressure. And after a short while, when the participant has "intrinsified" his part, he can recognize the bigger picture i.e., what the group is doing together.

The boomwhacker shows people some core elements of collaboration:

- The fact that we have to do it together.
- The fact that we have to have a common basic rhythm.
- The fact that we have to spread the task across people.
- The fact that we have to make sure that every individual task is not too complex so that the person doesn't need to constantly focus on his/her task but can also see where the others are and see the overall picture.
- The fact that every part is individual and unique.
- The fact that if individual parts change, the bigger picture can become even greater.
- And the fact that when we create something together, it becomes bigger than anything that you could create on your own.

The future can only be dealt with by working together. The more complex the world gets and the more challenging the world is, the more we need to understand that we can only achieve our goals (and survive) by integrating the vast diversity of different cultures, theories, behaviours and backgrounds.

That is the nature of collaboration. But collaboration is not exactly the right word for what I am trying to say.

Cooperation is a better one because cooperation goes

beyond collaboration. I want to be clear about the fact that it is actually cooperation and not collaboration that we should aim for. In many companies that I came across, collaboration was one of the things they valued highly. This was true even at companies where the values had just recently been spelled out.

However, collaboration is something from the last century. The nature of collaboration is to work towards one goal. People stick to that goal and make the goal more important than the individual. Collectives collaborate.

The future of the modern workplace is not collaboration but cooperation. To cooperate means that there is a balance between the goal set for the group and the goals of the individual.

This is not about setting the individual goal over and above the common goal. It is about balance. In cooperation, people work together towards a common goal because their personal goals are smoothly incorporated into that process. In order to do this, you need to pay attention to their personalities, their talents, their needs and their personal goals. You have to make sure that these match with the overall goal. People want to get connected and cooperate within the umbrella of connectives.

Collectives collaborate! Connectives cooperate! Isn't it funny that we talk naturally about companies *cooperating* when they work together while we naturally talk about *collaboration* when it is a about employees working together? The idea of cooperation is to keep the identity and integrity of all partners alive. Consequently we need to talk about cooperation.

A company that truly fosters cooperation will keep that in mind and avoid all means that force people into action by comparison, judgement, regulation, control and command. In other words, it will avoid internal competition and empower people instead.

This leads me to the third and most important quality of successful companies. Keeping music as a metaphor for life, it is the nature of a live music concert that will help us reveal that third quality.

By distributing the drums and establishing the first groove, we have established the "rhythm group" of our agile live band.

With the boomwhacker instruments, we have collaborated and added melody and harmony to the concert. But we haven't cooperated yet.

Rhythm, harmony and melodic instruments can create a decent song. But whether this performance is going to touch us or not is a completely different question. Because when we go to a live concert, the moment when we feel touched is not when the band delivers a song as we know it from the CD or streaming services. It's the moment when one of the instrumentalists takes his or her instrument, comes to the front of the stage and contributes something special, something unique, something that only he or she can play at that very moment. Doing this is only possible if the performer is willing to expose and open up his or her heart and soul to the audience.

It's quite important to look at how a great band behaves while one of their musicians is playing a solo. They know that they need to have that individual contribution and they know that their job is to create the basis and foundation to empower the soloist.

If you try to translate what we just saw in a band to a business, then the job of a corporation is not only to act agile and collaborate, but also to cooperate by paying attention to the potential and individuality of each person. It is the capacity of individual performance to reach greatness that makes the corporation's results stand out from the mainstream. But it's also important for the group to respond to that individual contribution with acknowledgement and appreciation.

Companies can create a field where employees gain the courage to stand up and say, "Hey! Here is something that I think only I can contribute to this situation, because it is something very personal for me." That would lead to cooperation.

Enthusiasm for the achievement of the organization as well as the individual are both required.

To make that tangible, we teach our audiences to play a solo too. The solo is made up of three different pieces. Once we have it set up and delivered, we're always missing something fundamental to the scene. We're missing that acknowledgement and appreciation. We're missing appropriate applause.

To get that into play, we split the group and make one side the audience and the other side the performers. The group watching the solo of the second group has the job of giving them a round of applause.

In the 2,800 events that I've done so far, I have only experienced unconditional appreciation twice. That was with a very special and unique management team of a company working in wildlife protection and it was a government job agency outside Germany. It touched me deeply.

In all other cases, the first applause given to the other side did not match the level of performance of the people. Because, by the time the solo happened, we had only had 45 minutes together. It was as though the participants hammered out this great and rather complex solo out of the blue. But the applause given, although nice, was not in keeping with how extraordinary the solo was.

What holds people back from giving this performance the applause that it deserves? There are plenty of misleading cultural mind-sets that could be brought up to explain this. But instead of talking about it, we just flip the groups. Those who have been the audience now become the soloists. For those who are now the spectators, we ask them to join in the experiment of giving the soloists the biggest applause they've ever given to any person yet.

Then we get it going. The second group plays the solo, and when it is finished, the audience stands up, cheering, whistling, clapping and jumping up and down. What you see in the faces of the people receiving that applause are shining, happy eyes. They are overjoyed.

Last but not least, what makes a company successful is that kind of enthusiasm for individual contribution. It is a culture of appreciation, acknowledgement and excitement about how special we are. And creating shining eyes is a very good plan for daily achievement.

The day when you haven't created a single pair of shining eyes is a day when you should consider what you can change tomorrow.

On the other hand, you may have an atmosphere that does not support individual contribution. You may not encourage people to talk strategy or you might respond that things have never been done that way. In this case, any individual who has brought up a new idea will step back and think, "Okay, I'm not stupid enough to expose myself and get treated that way again."

But just as a live concert without a solo is not touching, a company which doesn't encourage individual participation will not get a positive reaction from clients. Whether you're in a leadership position in a company or a leadership position in life, you can't achieve anything special by just following conventions rather than creating a field for people to stand up and make an outstanding personal contribution.

I had one client who was actually very well-positioned.

It was in the robotics industry and he had an absolutely amazing product that was setting him up perfectly for things to come. We did an event together. The CEO of the company approached me after the show and he asked for feedback about his company. I responded, "Well, if you ask me, then I have to tell you that I have seen companies that are not as great as yours. But at the same time, they celebrate themselves twice as much as you do. I see that as the biggest problem of your company. You do great things, but you do not acknowledge them well. And if that is the atmosphere at your company, you are probably doomed."

This was a couple of years ago and the company has now been sold to an Asian firm. And it's a shame that this had to happen, because enthusiasm is something that could have helped them move forward, especially when the going got tough.

I am absolutely convinced that you need the following things if you run a company:

- a sense of agility which means just doing it, without thinking too much.

- a culture of cooperation, which means truly working together towards a common goal but also seeing the individual and incorporating personal development, people's needs, what people love doing as well as their personalities and talents, and

- an atmosphere of enthusiasm and respect in everything you do.

Then it doesn't matter whether you produce pullovers, mobile phones or serve an IT infrastructure. You will be successful in everything, even your personal life.

When you're faced with a complex task (and I mean complex, not cumbersome) then face the challenge, seek a group to work with and do it together. Listen to individual ideas, succeed and show enthusiasm when you see the result. If you do this, you will always be successful.

A culture of appreciation and acknowledgement is the most important component of your company.

One day, I had the honour of talking about appreciation at the German Depression Congress, where 1,200 people, all directly or indirectly affected by depression, were present in the room. During the solo piece, after the second attempt with the huge applause, I heard a comment which I had often heard before. And this comment was, "Well, we deserve this increased applause only if we perform well. If our drumming had not been good, then we would not deserve this applause!"

The situation was so relevant that it made me do something I had not done before.

I asked the participants to remain in two subgroups. This time there was no drumming, but they were just requested to look at each other. They turned around on their chairs so that each group was facing the other, and everyone looked for eye contact with one person from the opposite side. They just looked into their eyes.

I walked behind one group and counted four, three, two, one, just with my fingers, without saying a word, because it was important to remain absolutely silent. On zero, the group on the other side gave exactly the same amount of applause that was given earlier, after the drumming. But now, the group on my side received it for doing nothing.

You deserve applause for just being who you are and what you are. You don't have to deliver anything important in order to deserve applause from other people.

I did this for the first time, and it was one of the most touching experiences I've ever had. I saw a house full of people in tears. Because they realised that this was touching their souls. This was important. This way of dealing with each other can help us fly.

The dynamics of that day made me really curious, because when this group received applause for doing nothing, they responded with applause in return. Which means they gave their neighbours applause in return for applause. This means that it is not necessary to be a rocket scientist to deserve applause. It means that it is enough to be kind to receive applause.

You can receive applause for your normal behaviour and not only for your achievements and peak performance.

This proves that if you give something good to the world, then you'll receive something good in return. The fact that people are giving applause in return for the applause they received is what I call Applause Culture 2.0 since that day.

When we think about the workplace 4.0, digitalization, automation and how we can survive as human beings, then the answer is Applause Culture 2.0. It is all about humanity, and it is all about seeing a person as an individual instead of using that person like an object in order to achieve something.

By that point of time in our sessions, most people have understood the meaning of applause. In real life, we may not treat ourselves that way. It would cause some confusion if everything we did required some hilarious freaking out. But we need to train ourselves and go a bit beyond normal, just like we do at the gym. We add some additional weight to the bar while lifting and this helps us to perform better in normal life.

We can do something similar when it comes to our applause for each other. In real life situations, this just means that we should show some more kindness to each other. Give the other person a smile, a good morning, an open ear, our presence, a clap on the shoulder, patience for one more second or a friendly word. We know how good this feels from our applause experiment and it alters our standard behaviour.

This is often reaffirmed in sessions when we introduce the applause culture as a warm-up to outcome presentations at the end of an extended Drum Cafe Academy workshop. Carried by the experience of Applause Culture 2.0, our tailored Pecha Kucha style presentations (five standardized slides presented for a total of five minutes sharp) create a stage energy for the presenter that you normally only expect from product launch events run by firms like Tesla or Apple.

And weeks later, clients tell us they still recall our approach when other presentations happen. "Do you remember that workshop recently with Applause Culture 2.0?" they ask, "Why don't we do that today?"

The one thing that remains to be said is that this applause culture is not only a culture of those giving applause but also of those receiving it. Sometimes, it's not easy to take credit for things. So we tend to trivialize the situation by saying things like "Ah, don't worry, that goes without saying" or the equivalent. But when we really think about it, then this is an act of disrespect against the effort the other person is making to say thanks or appreciate our work.

Even those who are used to applause have to deal with that tendency in their reactions. The movie, *This Is It,* is about a tour that Michael Jackson had planned. Unfortunately, it had to be canceled because of his untimely death. In the movie, you see that even one of the most professional stage performers in the world had to rehearse showing respect to the applause given. There is a scene at the end of one song where he stands still in his typical MJ pose, arms spread left and right at stage centre. And you hear the conductor repeating off-stage, "Hold for applause... hold for applause..."

In case you still have a feeling of awkwardness for this

kind of applause-giving experiment, you may consider this: Mark Twain said, "You should never regret anything that made you smile." The people in all our sessions were smiling and laughing. There was never anything to regret.

Albert Schweitzer mentioned something that I consider even more important with regard to this way of life. He said, "Nobody grows old merely by living a number of years. Yes, sooner or later, we'll see wrinkles on our skin. But when we avoid kindness and appreciation and fun and laughter in our day-to-day living, then it will cause wrinkles on our souls. We grow old by deserting our ideals."

Agility, cooperation and enthusiasm are a very good foundation for making a corporation successful. They also help the corporation to become a workplace that people would like to work at.

Chapter 4 (D#)
Inner Connections

Success is what follows when you follow yourself. You may want to change what's happening outside, but what you need to do is look inside yourself. With the three necessary qualities of corporations identified, it is worth looking at some matching inner qualities of people.

There's a famous HR magazine in Germany called *Manager Magazine*.

A couple of years ago, that magazine had its 25th anniversary, and, in order to honour that event, the front page featured the cover of the first issue 25 years ago. In his editorial, the chief editor wrote some words about how funny it was that when they looked at the cover of the first issue all those years ago, the topics and headlines were quite similar to those you saw today.

Little has changed regarding the pressing questions of leadership models, flexible work times, work-life balance, learning models, efficiency, change, burnout (which was not called burnout 25 years ago but was still a topic of importance), participation, gender and income neutrality as well as matrix management.

Today, the main issues may seem to be digitalization and automation. But the core questions behind these have been present for a long time.

I know the editor-in-charge and when we met at a fair, I told her that what she had written in her editorial did not seem that strange to me. Because if you take a technical magazine and compare one of its recent cover pages with one from 25 years ago, then you'll see that the topics and issues of the past were solved long ago, and we have moved on to other challenges by now. But in people development, strangely enough, there hasn't been much movement.

What is it that we're missing in our people development programs? In the chapter before, I was talking about agility, enthusiasm and cooperation as qualities of successful companies. One way or the other, this is very much what we focus on when we train people to become experts and leaders.

We develop agile work processes. We think about how we can structure and organise collaboration (yes, still collaboration, not cooperation). We create enthusiasm by offering competitive income packages, incentives and compensation models. Then we avoid thinking about what we're compensating for with these things. Why do we have to try so hard to keep people happy in our businesses?

There's a second layer underneath corporate qualities, which contains corresponding employee qualities. We need to understand these qualities and incorporate them into our people development programs.

Peace is the first quality.

I'm not talking about world peace or any kind of outer peace since that is out of our control anyway.

I'm talking about inner peace.

The question is: how do I deal with the realities happening in this world while still maintaining my freedom to decide and my ultimate self-responsibility—my awareness, my consciousness and my mindfulness? It's a question of whether I'm willing to spend time to develop mentally in order to become more balanced in dealing with challenges. Can I stay relaxed and calm instead of responding to everything that happens as though it were an emergency?

Joy is the second quality.

And again, it is not about external stimulation but the motor of inner joy. I'm also not talking about people plastering a great big grin or an artificial smile on their faces. I'm not talking about reframing everything that happens into a positive statement.

We know that we are sometimes faced with challenges that are not positive, funny or nice. We are faced with things that are actually quite disturbing and nerve-wracking and really bad. When I talk about inner joy, I am referring to the ability to enjoy the little things in life and gaining strength from them. I am talking about the ability to decide that I can summon the power needed in order to help me go through a bad situation.

Here is a picture I often use in my speeches to explain inner joy.

Imagine it is 10 o'clock in the morning. You are standing on top of a mountain and having your favourite hot morning drink—a good cup of coffee or tea. The weather is just perfect, around 22 degrees Celsius, with perfect blue skies and a mild breeze. You see a hawk circling up in the air. The world feels complete, perfect and peaceful.

If you just close your eyes for a second and envision this, you will be able to feel the power and strength to be gained from such a perfect moment.

Now imagine a situation in life where you feel like you're stuck at the bottom of a well. Your feet are about five inches deep in mud. When you look up, you see steep walls which are 10 to 25 meters high. Up in the sky, you see nothing but grey, heavy clouds and the rain is coming down, all the way into the well, drenching you from head to toe.

If you feel like you are in such a situation in your life, remember that you have the ability to recall the feeling of that mountain situation, in order to give you the strength to get up that wall and survive. That is what I call the power of inner joy.

In real life, this means training yourself to recall positive stimuli, a process that will help you to feel intrinsic joy. This, in turn, will help you gain the power to get through severe challenges.

And, of course, if you manage to do this, you can move back to your usual behavior, which is more balanced. There's no need to smile and grin all the time, just for the sake of doing it.

In Germany, we have a saying which goes: "This person is acting full of peace, joy and pancakes." It's a rather ironic phrase used to describe a person whose attitude is always, "everything is nice and easy" while knowing very well that it isn't. That makes it a great opener for the third quality to be introduced, since this is literally how we're making our way through this world, at least subconsciously.

We want to have universal peace and expect the world around us to change. But it isn't changing. And we don't stop to think about where we could actually make a difference i.e., when it comes to inner peace.

We want to have joy and expect the world around us to provide it. But it's not happening, and we don't think about what we're actually able to influence: the level of joy we are able to feel inside.

Finally, we think about all the "pancakes" we deserve to compensate us for our exhausting jobs, families, friends and communities. The pancakes stand for our salaries, incentives and bonuses. They stand for the huge car that we have in front of the villa and our constant need for overwhelming praise. All these things matter so much to our ego which wants us to look great and be rewarded for the pain of doing things we actually don't want to do.

But a complete and independent life doesn't just consist of "peace, joy and pancakes."

Instead, you need to replace the pancakes with the third quality: love.

Love is a big word, I know.

I'm not talking about the love between partners or intimate love. I am talking about making the decision to love yourself and love what you do. This is the basis for being able to love others at all.

Why do these three inner qualities link perfectly to the three qualities of a great company? It's quite simple.

In a company that is very agile and that has employees trained in possessing inner peace, things become quite easy. Because these people will not see any change driven by agility as a danger to their personal lives. They have learned to deal with it; they have learned to calm down. They can focus on their self-responsibility and what they can do with it. They see that things are just happening and you can never control them.

These people will always look inside and look for how they can deal with a challenge instead of working against it, questioning, moaning and playing the 'me-me-me' game.

People skilled at developing inner joy are perfect matches for an enthusiastic company. Because both will serve each other. A company that has enthusiasm will always please people who welcome joy as a part of their lives.

At the same time, even a company can struggle sometimes, and just acting enthusiastic for the sake of doing so does not work well. In that case, if the company has enough employees trained with inner joy, they can then become the vessels of an intrinsic movement within the company. They can create enthusiasm within themselves and others. By doing this, they can help the company go through a crisis and return to enjoying the enthusiastic workplace once the company is back to normal.

Love, the last quality, is my favourite one. Love links perfectly to cooperation for a very simple reason.

If you wake up in the morning, look into the mirror and hate yourself and what you do, then why on earth should anybody enjoy working with you? Or enjoy living with you, for that matter?

Regaining your balance and starting to work on accepting yourself as well as accepting what you do and what your duties are is the absolute, fundamental basis of becoming the kind of person that others want to cooperate with. It also gives you the strength to change or leave a situation if accepting it won't work.

It is an inner game.

There's a nice method in our workshops through which we make people aware of the need to look inside.

Let's take the example of a body percussion event since it allows you to do the exercise with any group you want even without a rhythm instrument. In a body percussion event, I work with two sounds which are created by clapping and snapping. At one point, I take a flip chart and introduce a simplified music scoring system.

Writing down music is actually very simple. The higher the sound, the higher the dot climbs up the lines. Since we need just two sounds for this exercise, we draw just one horizontal line and put a solid dot below the line to indicate a clap and one above the line to indicate a snap. That way, we can write down the sound we play, but we don't necessarily indicate how fast we're going to play it.

Next, I introduce an empty circle equivalent to two full solid dots; solid dots are played twice as fast as the circle. So a string of circles over the line means clapping at a certain speed and a string of solid dots over the line means clapping at twice that speed.

That is all the theory we need to have in place in order to write the first groove on the flip chart. The groove is "We will rock you."

I do two or three more examples. Once the system is completely established and the vast majority of people understand how it works, I take a blank flip chart. I write a final example—a very simple one consisting of two solid dots below the line and two solid dots above the line.

Clap, clap, snap, snap, clap, clap, snap, snap...

Every person in the room is now at the stage where they're able to understand and play that.

I write down "clap, clap, snap, snap" but I play "clap, snap, clap, snap" instead.

I intentionally create an obvious mismatch between what is written on the flip chart and what I do.

This always gives rise to a reaction in the audience. At the very least, it leads to confusion. I've even had audiences of 2,000 people boo at me.

They feel like I established a relationship of trust with them and then, I tricked them. I didn't walk the way I talked. So the audience had to make a decision.

At this point, the audience can be divided into three different groups: those who stick with what is written, those who flip and go with me and those who completely stop and take the position: 'I'm out.'

I stop the groove after a while and turn to the audience to gather the emotions that came up the very moment the mismatch occurred. I'm not interested in the facts, since I knew that I was doing something wrong. I'm interested in the emotions.

People start naming things like confusion, mistrust, self-doubt, loss of confidence, sometimes even anger.

I have just done one simple thing wrong: I didn't do what I communicated in writing. But, by doing this, I created all these strong emotions. I put them all down on the flip chart.

We all know that when we communicate with people, we don't only do so by telling them what we think or writing that thing down. We also communicate by choosing the words we say. We communicate via our body language. We communicate via eye contact. The pitch of our voice also helps us to communicate between the lines. So it is by all these means that we communicate.

But there are two more levels of communication that I think are completely underestimated. Communication also takes place at the level of emotions and beliefs.

Emotions and beliefs, especially the ones you are not aware of, get communicated all the time and in parallel to what you intend to communicate. You can call it subconscious behaviour if you like. It's also a result of empathy on the part of the recipient.

The message of my clapping-snapping experiment is that when you are not congruent in your communication, you create a gap. And this triggers all kinds of strong and dysfunctional emotions, not only in the case of an obvious mismatch between writing and doing but also in the case of a mismatch between saying and believing or expression and emotion.

If you get in front of a group of people and you think you have to play a role or put on a mask to get a certain message across—a message that is not truly yours—then people will recognise when you have doubts or when you get emotional. They will also react accordingly.

However, in real life, the effect is subtle and the feedback you receive will not be as strong as the feedback in our session. It's more likely that people will turn around and start talking behind your back when they're at the water cooler. And they'll basically be saying that something feels wrong with you or your company.

If you want to become an authentic person and leader, then you need to start opening up to look inside yourself. You need to start digging for your old and unexpressed bad feelings, your hidden beliefs and your pre-conditioned mind-sets. You need to tidy up that hidden mess and the process starts with becoming aware of it.

If you trick yourself, you'll trick others. There is a certain need to become conscious and aware. This applies to any employee of a successful company.

You need to understand that human resource development may have been limited in the past. You need to understand the fundamentals of authenticity. You also need to understand that everything depends upon your own mental development and the mental development of the people you lead.

You need to understand the challenges to come. You need to understand that we may be focusing on metrics to control our life, but the world will remain difficult and uncontrollable.

You need to start taking control of your reactions. By

doing this, you'll stop compensating but trigger real inner development instead. And this will help you to deal with what the so-called VUCA world is bringing us.

Sometimes, when I tell people this, they respond, "If I follow myself, I won't stay in that company." Maybe that's the way it is. But so what? You only have one life to live.

In any case, it's not good for the company either, to have employees who can't put their heart and soul into their work.

Some years ago, I had a conversation regarding sales with someone in a high-level management position of a huge German bank. He wanted to understand how I work. The question in the air was how I would deal with one specific person who'd refuse to participate in the drumming workshop and chose to block it out instead.

In response, I literally explained all of the means in place to invite that person to join, from the qualities of our program (which I have already explained) to the qualities of our facilitation (which I will explain in the chapters to come). They wanted to know how, specifically, I would react to such a person to keep things constructive.

It was a long conversation and we went deep into the characteristics of that person. We got to the point where all the managers concluded that the behaviour of that person simply indicates a very special nature.

They all felt that he has a tendency to disrupt for the sake of being disruptive.

I took a deep breath, and I said, "Well, then you had better fire him. Because if he's not doing something which all of you have agreed to pursue for completely valid reasons, then he's probably not the right person for you."

There was a short silence in the room and they said, "Well, we know that. But we cannot afford to get rid of him."

As a matter of fact, this is what happens sometimes. We are going through a time of major change and our decisions set the pace for the future. No one can hide from the transformative power of today. The world has never been changing as fast and as fundamentally as it is right now. Hence the need for people to adapt, change and develop. Deciding not to decide does not serve the company, nor does it serve the needs of the individual.

We need to develop ourselves and the people around us to become better human beings.

There is a great pool of possibilities to get that journey started, and each individual or organisation has to find their own unique start. With Drum Cafe and the Academy, we provide the positive experience of having made music together and the idea of the six qualities. We offer to take the group into a World Cafe workshop. We let them reflect on how they felt those qualities in the music and how many of them they can adopt into their lives and companies. What blocks us from adopting these qualities?

The outcome is always specific and always amazing. I once met with a bunch of about 60 really tough IT project managers. These were people who were doing really huge and demanding projects. They invited us for a full-day workshop on how to translate the togetherness in the music into day-to-day business life.

After making music, spending some time in the creative session of World Cafe, putting all the information together and boiling it down to a single line, those managers, who had been successful but also experiencing burnouts, depression and loss of employees on a massive level, boiled things down to this single line as a motto for the future:

"We need to strike a balance between money and love."

If I had entered the room as an external consultant, confronting these guys with this type of management model, it wouldn't have worked. But they came to that conclusion on their own, after reflecting on an experience. They created little place cards with that line to put on their desks, to remind them of a better future. It wasn't the end of the process, but it made a great start.

This is so fundamental and touching that it shows exactly how far the experience can go. There is only one thing in life that we have 100% control of, and that is how we react to things. We need to develop our inner strength to prepare for a changing world, or we become victims.

You may spend time to assess where you stand in terms of inner peace, inner joy and inner love. Would it make sense to you to open up to the contemplative arts and start looking for means to develop your mental strength?

My history and work have shown me how playing music together has made even hardliners recognise the gifts that come with maintaining connectedness. It made me and many of my clients incorporate a sense of spirituality into our lives to improve the ability to connect with ourselves and others. This helps us to develop as individuals and, in consequence, leads to more stabilised, complete and powerful teams and companies.

But before we start talking about contemplative arts and even "spirituality," it makes sense to take a look at your reptile brain.

Chapter 5 (E)
Brain Connections

You want your brain to perform, but first, you need to acknowledge its ancient parts which work unconsciously.

A massive amount of material has been released in the last few years about how the brain works, and neurobiology is taking huge steps forward. Just referencing all the advancements in this field would take up several books. Instead, I have prepared a brief summary that links to the experience of how people did in the Drum Cafe events for your personal consideration.

We need to understand the limits of our cognitive development and increase our overall brain capability by understanding that we can influence how our brain is changing. That thing that has altered common sense in the last five years is called neuroplasticity.

This means that we can change the patterns in our head in a deeper and more fundamental way than we thought we could in the past. And we can do this by changing our behaviour and actions.

Understanding this fact and starting to accept how much we're under the control of our old brain sections and unconscious patterns of thought helps us to understand that we need to get active and work towards positive change.

We can perform a funny little experiment to help us realise how little we control our brain when we don't have proper training.

Imagine you're sitting in a car and you feel a little urge to go to the bathroom. While you're driving, you read a sign stating that the next bathroom will come in ten kilometers.

You usually don't have any problem waiting that long. After all, you're not desperate to go to the bathroom yet. Even if there's a traffic jam after one kilometer, you're generally able to deal with it for a while because it is what it is. You may feel a little bit of stress about the situation but not much.

Now imagine you are at home and you have exactly the same level of pressure to go to the bathroom. This time, the bathroom is around the corner and you can reach it straightaway. You immediately proceed to the toilet, unzip your trousers and sit down. But you decide to break, stand up, zip up your trousers again and walk away, planning to return in five minutes.

Now, think about how that would feel. It is almost impossible to leave that bathroom because the need to urinate now seems more pressing than ever before. I suggest you really try it yourself to feel it. Biologically, there's no difference between both situations. It's not like there was so much more urine in your bladder in the second scenario. But the simple thought that you were physically able to go to the toilet in that moment created an unbearable amount of pressure.

If you can't make your brain relax and get back to the state of mind you had on the highway, you have to accept that you don't have much control over your brain at all.

You are much more steered by unconscious thoughts of ancient parts of your brain and by what you call "experience" than you would like to believe. It makes you blind to some extent.

The way I show that to people is through a little experiment I call the bicycle experiment. You can search on the Internet for the "bicycle pulling puzzle," and you'll see a full description of all the effects. The piece that we're using for our events is the version with a standard bicycle and standard gears or no gears at all. The types of brakes and freewheel function makes no difference. We hook up a rope to the pedal that is positioned at six o'clock.

We ask people what they think the bicycle is going to do if we pull that rope backwards horizontally. The classic first reaction is to say the bicycle is going to fall either left or right because it has no stand. Given that this is true, we posit that there is a virtual person standing next to the bicycle, keeping it straight but not

moving it in any way. This way, the bicycle is given the chance to react freely to the force coming from the rope which pulls the pedal backwards.

Then we ask people to have a one-minute dialogue with their neighbours to exchange opinions on what the bicycle might do.

Interestingly enough, the conversations don't stop after the minute is over. The results are not as obvious as people thought they would be. So they continue arguing about it.

Then we give them three possible outcomes to choose from. One is that the bicycle goes straight forward. Second is the exact opposite which is that the bicycle goes straight backwards. The third option is anything in-between those two extremes. For example, the bicycle could go a little bit forward and then backwards. Or it could just stand still. Or it could jump up and down. All these possibilities fall under option three.

We create an opinion poll in which people can vote for one of the three options. Until now, I've never had more than 10% of a group predict the outcome right. The one group that came up to 10% was a group of ten people, meaning that only one person had put up his hand. The bigger the group, the more the results tend to stay between 2-8%.

The interesting part is that the bicycle will actually go straight backwards.

This is always the time when people realise with a smile that I'm not just giving a motivational speech. My speech is meant to make people think. This is needed because over 90% people predict the wrong outcome.

I mentioned the full "bicycle pulling puzzle" video on YouTube because, if you are into physics, you'll see there that it is possible to have a situation where the bicycle moves differently. That technical extreme of special gearing is not the point of this whole experiment.

It gets most interesting when you look at how people predict the reaction if they have never seen a bicycle before. With no exception, those groups predict the outcome correctly 100% of the time.

- People who know a bike: +90% wrong.
- People who don't know a bike: 100% right.

That very difference is the point of the experiment. The second group is not thinking in terms of previous experience, gears, chains and the physics of forces. For these people, a bicycle is just a black box. It's just something that you hook a rope up to. And then, you pull the rope backwards. This makes the question almost trivial. What on earth can a black box do but follow the force coming from a rope being pulled backwards?

I demonstrate that on stage with my drum. There's a rope hooked up to my drum to help me carry it. You see me standing there, a drum on the ground and a rope attached to the drum in my hand. Then I ask people what would have happened if I had opened my speech with this question: "Here's my drum and here's a rope attached to my drum. If I pull the rope, then what do you think the drum is going to do? Is it going to come to me or is it going to go in the other direction? Or will it stand still or jump around?"

This has a jaw-dropping effect, because people realise how obvious and easy the answer really was.

So how come more than 90% are predicting the answer based on rather complex considerations like the propulsion system chains? That's because they're still thinking the way they did when they were learning to ride a bike. Look back to when you were five, six or seven years old. Maybe your uncle, aunt, parents or friends kept telling you that if you put power to the pedal, you would move forward.

There's little in this world that has been hammered into our brain structure as much as this effect. Because of that, we don't see the obvious. Something gets dragged somewhere, so it goes there. Period.

Besides, when you are sitting on a bike and you're pressing the pedal with your foot, then you are moving forward, together with the bike. You're inside the system. You are not applying a different kind of force to the bike from outside.

This is what increases the chances of your getting it wrong.

In this way, I explain why we have brought these musical instruments. They're not there for the sake of making music and having fun with each other but to make the people in the room face a new system.

That bicycle puzzle demonstrates that when you are in the systems that you know best, it is most likely that you will get blinded by your experience. A system you don't know is the perfect start for some really new learning experiences. Hence the music.

Making music together is much better than trying to understand my client's business and talking about it. Because when it comes to business, people already have a number of preconceived notions. As a result, there's little chance of change.

That is how much existing brain connections override the novel thinking that we attempt. As a result, we must force ourselves to create new brain connections actively. It's a fact that the human brain hasn't changed much biologically in the last 10,000 years.

Our brains just got better by connecting more! Our development of the last 10,000 years is a cultural one, not a biological one.

In this way, the brain showcases a healthy way forward.

It's all about getting connected better. It's not about doing bigger things.

We have certain areas in our brain that deal with survival, satisfaction and solidarity—the three drivers of our current behavior. It astonished me to see how they link quite perfectly to the three qualities of companies, as mentioned in chapter 3 and the three qualities of human beings which are mentioned in chapter 4.

The survival centre creates those flight, fight or freeze reactions when faced with danger. And when there is change, it interprets it as danger. This results in fear instead of working hand in hand with the agile world. But this fear can be relieved when you train yourself to create inner peace.

The satisfaction centre is also our internal gratification centre; it provides us with a lot of really great feelings by releasing hormones in moments of excitement. Unfortunately, it is also the area that can be stimulated quite easily from the outside by owning possessions and doing drugs. If it is only stimulated in this negative way, this leads to attachment and greed within the individual. It takes longer to stimulate this centre via intrinsic motors like inner joy.

The centre of solidarity is the one that makes us seek connectedness with other beings. It gives us the stimulating feeling of being part of a group. On the positive side, it helps us cooperate with others through acts of love. We express love for others and others love us back.

However, this centre is much abused in the history of Germany and many other places in the world. It is the motor of very negative group dynamics which result in laziness and selfishness. When this happens, people forget that the purpose of life is to act for the good of yourself *and* others.

Fear, greed and laziness are three rather dark forces that we have to overcome. We can do so by taking action and via contemplative practice.

Playing a drum makes a person step out of their comfort zone. It creates new links in the brain. So it is a contemplative practice on its own.

We need to keep in mind that neuroplasticity exists; you can change your brain by changing your behaviour. Contemplative practice is a solid way of doing this, but it needs time. You need about 8-12 weeks of practice in order to feel the effects. That applies to any new behaviour or habit and especially to any training to increase consciousness and mindfulness.

There is a very nice way in which we convey this to groups. We make use of the boomwhacker instruments again, but, this time, I ask people to do a little experiment with us before playing.

I invite them to do a little bit of meditation with me by not thinking of anything for the duration of one minute. There should be no thinking at all, not even thinking about not thinking. This means you can't repeat "I'm not thinking" in your head. Because that would be thinking as well.

After one minute, I ask the audience if any of them has been able to think of nothing for the full duration of time. The response I get is that maybe two out of 100 have managed to think of nothing. The rest weren't able to switch off their brains. And I personally think that, in most cases, those two haven't been able to succeed either as it is extremely difficult to force your mind not to think.

For the moment, I leave the audience with that experience. Yes, it is hard to switch off the brain. It might do us a lot of good, but it just won't stop operating.

With the boomwhacker, we start a rumble of all tones. Then we introduce the rumble in individual tones. In a pentatonic scale, the keys that correspond to these tones are C, D, E, G and A.

Once we have introduced all the single notes, we play a piece of music on an audio player or we have the percussionist(s) tune in. We play a nice melody using the boomwhacker, first with single notes, then by introducing very pleasant intervals and playing two notes at the same time. All this leads up to a finish with a boomwhacker rumble by the whole group.

Four-three-two-one-stop. We come to a complete halt.

We reflect on what just happened. First of all, we played a nice melody—an amazing tune that touched people and felt relaxing. But there's yet another point that's more important.

I ask people if anyone in the room has thought about anything else but what we just did for the duration of the three or four minutes we just spent making music. Did they have any exhausting thoughts about work, open issues, money or any other challenges in their lives?

In response, only two or three hands go up out of 100.

Making music turned the situation upside down. We went from a situation where it was hard to switch off your brain and stop thinking to a situation where it was hard to think of anything at all.

I myself have made it a habit to try to think about

something strange or something intense that happened in my life just before getting into this experiment. And even though I tried to keep those thoughts in mind while drumming, I wasn't able to do so for longer than a couple of seconds. After that, I was making music with people. I was absorbed in the moment. Nothing else remained.

That is the first step which opens the door to a new experience. It's a way to get rid of the mind chatter—to stop all these thoughts.

Don't get me wrong. Thoughts and thinking are not bad. Thinking has brought us quite far as a culture and as human beings. But the problem with our brains is that it's hardly possible to stop these thoughts. Whenever we think we have stopped, we continue thinking about the past and what came before the stop. And as if that isn't enough, we start thinking about what's going to happen after the break. Our brain just never stops working.

But the thing is that it's very relaxing to the brain and also to the soul if we have the ability to make thinking stop on demand.

Years ago, I had a conversation with a Shaolin monk and he told me that this is the very reason why they have different types of activity in place like kata fighting, yoga, Qigong, t'ai çhi, cultivating bonsai and origami. These things make your body active and put you into a meditative state. Even for the Shaolin monks, meditation is hard. And switching off your brain just by looking at a spot on the wall is almost impossible.

But people might not have their origami materials or their boomwhacker or any other instrument with them in the moment. In that case, there's one little exercise that we can all do at any time. I call it a slo-mo meditation and it is based on a concept that Shi Shi Mink, the Shaolin Monk told me.

Whenever you feel like you want to be connected with the moment and switch off your brain, continue doing whatever you're doing but do it in slow motion for 30 seconds, simply recognising what is around you.

Imagine you are in a meeting. Everyone is going berserk around you. And in that very moment, you decide to ease your brain by taking a break. You slow down and you pick up your cup of tea or coffee. Slowly, you move it towards your mouth. You feel the warm cup touching your lips and the liquid going down your throat and hitting your stomach. And while you do it, just breathe into your belly. Notice the way you sit, the temperature, the sounds, the smells and the vibes in the room. Recognize what you see but do not judge what you observe. That's all. After 30 seconds, just continue what you were doing before.

If you do that five times a day, then you're spending two and a half minutes in contemplative practice, which is not much. We're not talking about assigning two hours per day to a massive meditation practice. I ask you for less time than brushing your teeth—just two and a half minutes.

And the promise is that, after two or three months, your life is going to change. Because you're starting to train brain areas to do better.

You have that reptile brain—like the amygdala—that is very old and very quick. So whenever you're under pressure and you have to react very fast, it is that very amygdala, amongst others, that is going to react first. It is an old and *ad hoc* brain area that does not make the cleverest decisions.

But you have other younger areas, such as the pre-frontal cortex. This part of the brain is cleverer; it reacts more out of wisdom and knowledge. But because it is younger, it is slower than the amygdala. So whenever you feel tense or stressed out, the amygdala takes over and makes "old" decisions, such as fight or flight.

It has now been proven that two to three months of contemplative practice helps the neural connections in the pre-frontal cortex to grow and the ones in the amygdala to shrink.

By doing this, you can change how you perceive the world around you. You get more empathic and you perceive more things around you. If there's a person passing by on high heels on a stone floor (to pick up the metaphor alluded to earlier), then you may perceive that person even if you are in active mode at that very moment.

Our music sessions pull the vast majority of the audience into the present immediately. The answers to the biggest questions of our lives lie in the present. Yesterday is in the past, tomorrow is in the future, but today is a gift. That's why it is called the "present." You can train your brain to become aware of that. Your body is the bridge to the present.

"The art of resting in the present is part of the art of working," said John Steinbeck.

Chapter 6 (F)
Global Connections

Once you get in touch with what's happening in the present, you also become aware of how connected things are on a bigger scale.

Let me start with some important events—two professional and one private.

Bodo Janssen, manager of the hotel group Upstalsboom had the realisation that, in brief, he hadn't been a top manager at all, but rather a flop manager, as he stated later in his book, *The Silent Revolution* (*Die Stille Revolution*, unfortunately only available in German).

Chapter 13 of the book starts with a short recap of an event in March 2013 which was designed to create a new corporate model. To start the event, 80 managers experienced a Drum Cafe event which was intended to help people relax and understand the basics of cooperation and teamwork. The idea was that once people understood how these things worked in drumming, they would also be able to understand how they worked in day-to-day business.

This was the first day of a change that has become a legend in the German hotel industry and management literature. People are now treating each other differently in terms of humanity, purpose and their footprint in the world. And this is all due to the impressive social projects that Upstalsboom has put in place since that day. Changes in a hotel management room can change places in Africa.

The second event I'd like to reference took place at the end of 2016 with the Holtmann Group in Germany. As part of the year-end celebrations, we were drumming with staff, partners and employees of the company. At one point, we built up a wall made of Cajon instruments. A Cajon is a box usually made of wood and about 45 cm high. It's also called the smallest drum set in the world due to its amazing sounds when played as a hand-drumming instrument.

We used 35 paper versions of the Cajon and stacked them to form a wall. On the front of the instruments was a plain white sticker making this wall the presentation canvas for a video projector that evening. At some point in our performance, a group of refugees entered the room. They lived next to the headquarters of that company. They tore down that wall, and turned it into individual Cajon instruments to join the performance.

With that simple move, we brought different cultures together without speaking a single word. We did it via music and, while many people in the world currently talk about building walls in order to separate their country from neighboring countries, we demonstrated that tearing down walls and translating the process into togetherness and connectedness feels much better.

My third example doesn't come from music. It happened in the summer of 2011. It was a cornerstone in my life, when I realised that there must be more happening between people than our physical senses can capture.

My wife and I came back from a trip to Bimini where we had gone swimming with dolphins. The two weeks at the amazing retreat called "Wildquest—The Human-Dolphin Connection" has enough material for an entire book. It paved the way to a new life for me. But the best was saved for last when we returned.

Shortly after the plane took off, a person on board had a heart attack. We were too far away from Florida to get the plane turned around and fly back. And a doctor on board insisted that that person was in serious danger.

The captain made the decision to bring the plane down and land it at a rather small nearby airport. I didn't know how fast a plane could descend until that very day. But fortunately, they were able to get the patient to a hospital on that little island.

After this emergency landing, the plane did not have enough fuel to continue to Germany. And the airport where we landed was too small to allow the continental airplane we were in to take off with the weight of full fuel. In addition, the machine had to be checked by the manufacturer, because it had landed without fuel dumping; it had too much weight. Quite a few things had to be worked out before we could head off.

The 170 passengers on the plane were a mix of adults, kids and even little babies. The problem was that we had to remain grounded for more than six hours and were not allowed to leave the plane, since this would've taken us off "German territory." We did not fulfill the requirements to enter a foreign country, since there were no customs or immigration officials at this airport.

It was clear that even when things were sorted, we would proceed to another airport, stay overnight and get the plane checked and fully fuelled. This meant that we would have to stay even more time in the air en route to a place yet unknown.

Service was not the priority in the beginning when this happened, so there wasn't much going on inside the plane until, at last, some water was provided. The plane was also not stocked for the sheer length of the flight, which meant that everything was in short supply.

Since the man who had suffered the heart attack was seated just a few meters away from me, I was struck by having witnessed a person so close to death. But the cabin was huge, and there were also many people sitting far away who were not really aware of the details of that man's critical situation.

I assume you can picture the situation. And if I had imagined it in advance, I would have expected arguing adults and moaning kids all over the place.

But there was 100% silence in that cabin. From babies who should have been wailing to adults who were missing out on their busy schedules in Berlin, the crowd was perfectly calm, relaxed, understanding and patient. I've never seen this happen in any group I've been a part of. It felt like some kind of fundamental love in the air.

We ended up at a hotel in the Dominican Republic late after midnight. When we were finally back in the plane en route to Germany, I started reading a book. When I reached the end of a chapter, I looked up and saw the stewardess coming. I stopped her to ask how things had turned out and if the man had survived.

"Yes, he did and he's doing much better," she said.

I turned back to my book and flipped to the next page. The very first sentence of the next chapter was, "If you save a single life, then you actually save the whole world."

Suddenly, I found myself sitting on my seat in tears.

What do these three events have in common?

In all three cases, people were brought together on a very deep level, and this brought about some very touching and special moments. They stopped thinking about other people as objects used to achieve a certain personal goal. They recognized all human beings as important subjects aiming for personal growth while helping others to achieve a common goal and creating a meaningful existence for all of humanity.

Connectivity exists between all things on a global scale. We strive for technical connectivity, but we also need to open up for that deeper connection between all living beings that exists anyway.

Remember the movie *Avatar*? How about considering that the navigation system of our life involves understanding that we actually are the "Navi" ourselves?

Millions have watched *Avatar* and fallen in love with the Navi life forms and Pandora. They hate the intruders who don't see that, on this planet, everything—every being, every plant, every animal and every Navi—is connected. The intruders don't get that; they focus on business and economic success without realising that Pandora is a perfect place of universal connectedness. We sympathise with the Navi and want to send the intruders off-planet.

But when you take Pandora as a metaphor for the Earth and bring up the idea that we too might have that connectivity between all things, then people close their minds and say, "No, that's not possible. It's too spiritual."

I admit the last few paragraphs may sound spiritual and I have to say I'm an "engineering" kind of guy who is not really into those eerie kinds of things! But what does spirituality actually mean? To me, it is very simple. Spirituality refers to anything which you can't touch but which affects you all the same.

I have a thesis: there must be a reason why we, as human beings, are promoting stuff like digitalisation and the Internet of Things (IoT) so much. Both stand for the same thing: digitally representing and technically connecting each thing in this world, from mobile phones and information resources to social networks and the tree in the garden with its watering system.

My thesis is that the Internet of Things is nothing but a technical clone of a deeper truth. And that truth is that everything is connected, even if human beings are not willing to accept this as a phenomenon.

I think *Avatar* is one of the most successful spiritual blockbusters ever filmed on that subject. It deals with the question of spirituality and connectedness. We are not Dr. Grace Augustine, who discovers the planet and has the physical means to measure its connectivity. We cannot measure it. It's not tangible to us. We can only get a glimpse of a feeling here and there like I did in that plane.

Now, I see the reaction of thousands of groups to something that I once doubted myself and the reaction is decidedly positive.

Part of the Drum Cafe program is a short sequence of body massage. Now that the audience can drum, that movement of the hands can also be used to turn around and do a bit of "drumming" on their neighbours. It leads into a decent massage of the shoulders and upper back area. I mention it here in this book, but I don't tell my clients about it in the sales phase anymore because they invariably have doubts about it.

"Ask people to touch each other in a business scenario? No way!" Everyone thinks it is encroaching and is not going to work, especially at a professional event. If I had told them about it in advance, most clients would have asked me to skip that piece. Which would've been a mistake, as it is exactly that piece that provides a certain magic to the moment.

What I had to learn is that even the most critical and the most skeptical people—groups who appeared not to be connected at all—reacted positively to the massage. Once I asked them to relax their fingers after the first drumming, then turn right and give their neighbour just a little bit of a shoulder massage, the last pieces of ice broke away.

For some reason, we seem to be eager to get back that body contact mentioned in chapter 1. It might be hardwired in our brain due to experiences that we've had in the first nine months of our being i.e., that bodily connectedness with another person.

There must be a lot of truth in this idea, because in all the events that I did, there was not a single group that did not massively enjoy the massage. And the truth is, people won't stop once they have started. Funny, isn't it, when taking into account that my clients were usually not in favor of this part of the program? If I'd actively asked them for permission, I wouldn't have gotten it.

Here we see it nice and clear—the difference between what we want and what we need. We often don't have the slightest clue about what we are in real need of before we give it a try.

People get into body contact and subconsciously realise that touching each other is healing each other.

I urge you to start incorporating body contact—not just shaking hands but also hugging. Try to find a group of people that you can give a true hug to when you meet them.

This group doesn't have to be full of strangers. It doesn't need to include people that you have business relationships with. Start with the people that you're probably giving a hug to already. But in the future, give them a true hug, not just any hug. This means that you have to remain in that situation for a second and feel the connectivity between you and the other person.

To put it all together, I would like to bring up the thesis of non-duality which the classic mystics refer to as a state of enlightenment (Buddhist), a realisation of the true self (Hindu), or a divine oneness with the Godhead (Christian, Islamic and Jewish).

When the idea gets that big, I have a recommendation

about how to avoid becoming dogmatic about any approach. I see it as being similar to learning to cook. Because if you want to learn to cook, I think you would not look for the one and only cooking master in the world and then make him your shining guru, follow him step by step and copy exactly what he does. Because, by doing this, you can only become a complete clone of that cook, doomed to live in the shade of your master. Instead, you should practice your own version of cooking.

The way we learn cooking is rather diverse. We learn to fry our first eggs in a pan from our mums or dads in the early days. We just hang around watching and catch something on the run. If we are more deeply interested in cooking, we may one day start to do it in a more structured way. We may seek advice whenever we can. We may read a book or scan the web. We may take a cooking course or start an apprenticeship. We may get impressions and inspiration from all over the place, maybe even become a game changer in the kitchen.

At the very end, you become your own cook and you create the meals in a way that only you can. You express your true self in cooking.

The same applies to spiritual development. You pick things up as you go along. These are the things that resonate with you. The path to a reasonable spiritual life is diverse.

A good start is to bring "spirituality" down to

reasonable terms. For example, this can be done by acknowledging that music is spiritual by design as it cannot be touched, but it touches you. And by acknowledging that spirit exists in every moment and relationship. Even the "spirit of a company" is a spiritual topic.

"It is the relationship to other people that gives life its worth," says Humboldt.

In some way, we are all "one world, one pod" as stated on the webpage of Wildquest, the place I mentioned for swimming with dolphins that was the cornerstone of my personal change. And we all exist in relation to each other. It's about time we accepted this. It's about time we broke down some walls and borders like we did in that paper Cajon event in 2016.

In order to do this, we need some connectedness training.

Chapter 7 (F#)
Daily Connections

In "training," you make an active effort and assign time and energy towards rehearsing or repeating a certain routine in order to improve something. What we completely underestimate is how much better you learn without the pressure of "learning." This means that your unconscious but daily routines have the strongest effect on you in the long run.

It is important to shed some light on those routines. Because when you think you're intentionally training hard at activity "A", you're actually training yourself much better in activity "B" without even knowing it. I say that because the things that affect your training strongly become more apparent in hindsight.

For that reason, I don't want to provide you with new training routines in this chapter. Instead, I'd rather start an awareness process of what you are constantly training yourself to do in a subconscious way.

You become what you connect with. As a matter of fact, most people want to be informed about things and become complex individuals, but you need to be very selective and conscious about what you connect with on a daily basis.

There is a great African saying called Ubuntu. This means that we are what we are by virtue of the people around us.

In other words, the decision of what and who you connect with has a major effect on your future development.

To me, Ubuntu is actually more than a saying; it's a way of life. It doesn't only include the people that are around us, but everything that takes place around us. In one of my offerings to my clients, we help the participants to recognize how constant and subversive influences insidiously enter our lives.

Since music is my basis, I take our ears as the starting point. What I'm going to say applies to all our senses, but the ears are very special and unique organs; hearing is the only sense we have that we cannot switch off in public without causing irritation.

If there's something that you don't want to see, it is quite easy to look somewhere else or even close your eyes. In modern cultures, it is absolutely socially acceptable if you ask not to be touched by a person if you don't want it. And it's also possible not to touch a thing yourself if you don't want to. You can't be forced. It is socially acceptable to reject. You can also stop breathing through your nose and just breathe through your mouth if there is a smell that you don't like and literally no one in your surroundings will even recognise that you are protecting yourself at that moment.

But you're unable to close your ears, because your ears are constantly open, even when you are asleep. You have to make it really obvious if you don't want to hear something. For example, if someone is saying something that you don't want to hear, you can either leave the room or put your hands over your ears. Both actions are very visible to the person you're speaking with and can be taken as an affront.

In most cases, socially conditioned as we are, we stay in the room and let the words still have some effect as they sneak into our brains.

Go through something with me for a moment. This is something that we do in our sessions to make people aware. If you have a computer with web and sound available, you can get it set up before you proceed. If you don't have a computer nearby, don't worry. I'm going to describe the experience anyway.

Open your browser and enter the following line but do not hit start yet. Wait.

http://tcp-hearing-hygiene1.matthias-jackel.com

What I'd like to do first is a little bit of meditation, asking you to imagine a perfect day at the sea. You're on a white beach with clear water in front of you. You are standing barefoot in the warm sand. You have the drink of your choice in your hand. It's morning and your perfect spouse is having a swim. The weather is nice, the sky is blue and a mild breeze brings you the smell of the ocean.

Give yourself a bit of time to get into the picture.

Do not continue reading after the next line.

Once you are ready, after some time, click return on your computer to start the sound.

If you don't have a computer, the sound is a light Caribbean song known to most people in the world as the famous jingle of the Bacardi Rum commercials.

Even if you haven't seen the images used in those commercials, you still associate this specific kind of music with a party scene and very easy living.

Take a minute to let that sink into your imagination and then go back to the original scene you had in mind before the music started. Imagine the same time, same place and same situation with your spouse swimming in the sea.

When you are ready, enter the following line in your browser, hit return and, again, please do not continue reading.

http://tcp-hearing-hygiene2.matthias-jackel.com

The sound is the main theme of the famous movie *Jaws*.

In case you haven't seen the movie, that sound is the perfect tune to create horror in your imagination. It's not a stretch to imagine this piece of music playing while you're being attacked by a shark.

Look back at how the scenes changed in your mind. The simple choice of a sound effect has altered the imagination. That's how powerful hearing is.

And this is only a warm-up.

Here's the third clip that I present to my audiences:

http://tcp-hearing-hygiene3.matthias-jackel.com

Before you click return, make sure that you have about nine minutes of silence for yourself. Take a relaxed position on a chair or lie down on the floor. You'll hear a sequence of sounds taking you through a journey of the imagination. I invite you to let all mental images and emotions come up and flow freely in your mind.

Enjoy the process.

* * *

Done? Let me tell you what reactions I get in the live sessions. They may match some of yours.

The music is a set of nine jingles of different types. Some of it is party music and some of it is classical. There's a movie score and a relaxing piece of music. But then, these are replaced by the sounds of day-to-day life. One is applause. One is a street scene with many cars and lots of sounds—police passing by, a helicopter flying and people yelling. It is a hectic and stressful scene.

Then we play a jingle that is typically used on TV and radio while the news is reported. The jingle sets the pace to create fear, prepping your body for alarming news, even before the first word is said. When we think about the news which the media reports every day, we can safely say that most of it is very serious and very bad. Why on earth do they feel like it's necessary to also precede it with that alarming piece of music? Doesn't it make the process of hearing the news even worse?

There's a lot of intentional fear created in the minds of the audience. The music makes sure the news hits you harder than it would otherwise. It increases the intensity of the experience and enables the media to sell marketing slots at higher prices. It is a bizarre system.

Then we go over to the second-last sound, which is the ringing of a mobile phone. Here, at last, you see the physical reactions of people, because they're shivering and shaking. They realise that the simple sound of a telephone gives rise to a whole string of emotions and associations in their brain. And most of these associations are about work problems and work stress.

Recall what your first bodily reaction was when you heard the ringing in the sound clip. What if it had actually been the specific ring tone of your personal phone?

After this comes a scene of woods with birds and a piano playing in the background. It leads people back to a situation where they realise that connecting with the earth and a calming scene has a positive impact on their inner state of mind and their emotions.

Keep in mind that you can never close your ears. So sounds like these jingles influence you on a day-to-day basis.

You should know that the power of music is constantly used in public, from shaping your expectations when getting the news to making you buy products that you don't need. What adds to the intentional usage of sounds is the effect of the natural sounds surrounding you every day, from the relative silence at night to the street sounds during the day as well as the noise at your workplace and the tone in which people speak to you and each other around you.

What you need is to seek protection from that or at least to listen consciously. Seeking protection means that you should make the decision to seek silence whenever possible.

Next time, when you drive to work in the morning, make the decision to switch the radio station off. You may think you want to hear music, but what happens is that you hear the music that other people have selected for you and you also hear the commercials that go with the music. You hear the news that is announced after a piece of music. And if you have a longer ride to your workplace, then you may hear the news two or three times more often than you want to.

While you're going through the day, you constantly receive subliminal messages that have an infectious effect on the way you behave during that day.

Over the years, I've seen people getting connected

often and deeply. As a result, I have realised that we are seeking and absorbing connections like sponges collecting and absorbing water.

Simply because we're so hardwired for connecting and seeking connectedness with other people, we have to be very careful with what we connect with every day, not only through our ears, but also through all of our senses. What you read every day in the newspaper or what you watch on TV or what you listen to on the news has a dramatic effect on how you go through the day.

This constant, mostly unconscious, training effect is changing the way you perceive the world. You need to carefully consider what books you read and what movies you watch and whether listening to all the news in the world is going to support you in the purpose of your day.

I realised the magnitude of that myself many years ago when I was reading a newspaper article about the upcoming construction of the great A 380 airplane. Airbus Industries hired 10,000 people in their manufacturing area to get this done. There was a note in the newspaper on the second page stating that these 10,000 people had been hired. It was just a coincidence that a couple of years later, Airbus had to lay off 2,000 people because of some engineering problems they faced affecting delivery dates.

Incidentally, I had the same newspaper in my hand, both times. The information about the layoffs came on the front page. And, for the first time in my life, simply because I was so interested in the development of the Airbus A 380, I realised that hiring 10,000 people is news worthy of the second page while laying off 2,000 people is news worthy of the front page.

From that day onwards, I began to carefully watch how things are presented to me and I realised that there's a certain strategy in the way the news is shown, simply because bad news sells better. The purpose of the firms providing news is not to inform people in order to create a better world but to make money. The ethical question of journalism is not about being objective since subjects can never be objective. Good journalism should be driven by responsibility.

It was on a Sunday morning after a terrible bomb attack that I bought some rolls in a bakery. At checkout, I saw a popular Sunday newspaper. I looked at it and shook my head. The Arabian-born owner of the bakery said, "You know, this newspaper is creating more terror than the terrorism itself because the words they use are the wood behind the spearhead of the bomb."

What a wise man.

If you hear bad news every day because the mainstream media has decided to send it your way and you're not aware that there are other types of media which are reporting about positive things happening in life, then your perception of the world is probably not in balance and doesn't reflect reality.

The same applies to all the social media that you're on. As a matter of fact, all social media traces our behaviour. That means that what you connect with and the messages you repost or "like" drive social media to decide what messages you're going to be presented with on the next day. The success of social media is based on the fact that you share and distribute news and there is no reason why social media should give you a recommendation for news of the day if you don't retweet or repost or "like" or interact in any other way.

If you decide to share a story about a person doing something positive to the community, then this has a completely different effect on the behaviour of your social media compared to just sharing another "funny" video of a baby tripping over while playing.

My daughter once looked at my Facebook account and wondered why I was getting all these great messages whereas she gets a lot of crap day in and day out. We talked about it and she realised that it's because she's giving energy to that crap.

Facebook and similar services are nothing but a mirror of your behaviour. This is a great example that illustrates how you become what you think. You get what you dish out.

She decided to clean up her Facebook account and disconnect with the people who were sharing messages that she actually doesn't like. It felt really good to her.

We live in a world that is getting more and more connected electronically and I understand that there are people whose duties depend on being informed. This is true, and I know that there are jobs that require listening to the news. But if the information you take is primarily driven by social-media then this is especially dangerous. It is exactly that bias-based information providing technique of social media feeds that makes biased people even more biased. The idea of the information provided is not to give you a wider scope but to feed you with what you like already. This is the opposite of developing open-mindedness and globally a big issue, considering the impact social media has.

When I was young, we had two TV channels, the radio and the local newspaper and we were compelled to take what those services provided. Today, we have more choices. With those choices comes the ultimate freedom to decide what we hook up to. And with freedom comes responsibility. The art is to seek the right mix of sources and to be aware that there are also news sources available on the Internet that do nothing but share positive news.

As a start, consider some of these ideas and sources that happened to be very inspiring to me.

Instead of opening the newspaper or switching on the TV first thing in the morning, start your day with a moment of silence and connection with yourself.

Instead of listening to the radio on your way to work, I recommend silence again or using a streaming service that provides the music that you want with no commercial interruption.

I know that it's great to watch TV for relaxation. There's absolutely nothing wrong with that. But are you enjoying the positive relaxation effect of watching an inspiring movie? Or are you just switching on something, compensating for a bad day, flipping through TV channels and digesting all the commercials coming through? If so, then your experience turns into massive brain-washing created by a mix of bad news, bad ideas and bad "must-haves" while you continue to think that you're relaxing.

Instead, do it consciously. Select a movie of your choice, make the decision to enjoy it and use a streaming service or a DVD with no commercial breaks. Good movies have a certain message that can be broken down into very few words, sometimes just one word.

I mentioned *Avatar* earlier. To me, the one word that describes this movie is "non-duality." Or watch *Peaceful Warrior*. To me, the one word that describes this movie is "self-trust." I also watched this beautiful movie while I was writing this chapter: *Three Billboards Outside Ebbing, Missouri*. To me, it's all about "forgiving."

Consider replacing just one routine per day. Instead of watching a soap opera, watch a TED talk at *www.ted.com*.

Instead of consuming the Sunday press, I recommend magazines like *Happiness* or *Moment-by-Moment* (both available in Germany only) or an English version like Positive.News (www.positive.news) that focus on reporting positive things and envisioning a positive future.

Instead of receiving daily pop-ups from standard internet news services, add some daily messages from positive news services like *Perspective Daily* or *Newslichter* (both available in Germany only) or use designated areas of *Huffington Post* like

> http://www.huffingtonpost.com/topic/power-of-humanity

> or

> http://www.upworthy.com

> or

> http://www.goodnewsnetwork.org

Instead of reading fiction books only, I suggest adding some books that come from, and deal with, real life. My personal favourite? *Search for Meaning* by Viktor Frankl. I also recommend reading texts and publications by Marshall B. Rosenberg about nonviolent communication as well as the many inspirations available by book and web sources from Siddharth Gautama (the Buddha), Osho, Yongey Mingyur Rinpoche, Rumi and the Dalai Lama. I leave it with that start of my favourite ones as this list could go on for pages, the reviewing and reading of which could lead to an obsession by itself.

So, lastly, avoid any attachment with the material you consume.

It was the Dalai Lama himself who said, "Things are made for being used and humans are made for being loved. The chaos in the world comes from the fact that we love things and for that, we use people."

Your daily connections should be with diverse and positive people, not with things.

Chapter 8 (G)
Human Connections

What does good communication between human beings consist of? That's like asking: what's the best move in chess? The answer is that it all depends on where you are in the game. There is no one single move that will always lead to success in every situation. You just need to react flexibly depending on what's going on. In order to get good at the game, you need to love the game and dig deeply into it. Similarly, out of the vast amount of communication that's going on in the world, I'd like to focus on some specific types that appear relevant to me.

The underlying question of all communication is: do you actually enjoy being in contact in that moment? Your consciousness will tell you that everything on this planet changes from time to time. What you enjoy and what seems easy to do in one moment may seem tough and exhausting at another moment in time.

Sometimes, you may want easy relationships and things; you may want concepts that work right away.

But what you *need* may be something quite different. You may need depth, diversity and growth. Being able to work in these diverse states of mind will enable you to get into better and more stable relationships. It will enhance the trust between you and others.

Step one is to develop the curiosity to meet people with openness and to let go of any expectations.

Over the years, I developed a basic attitude that worked any time I was meeting a new group of people. Many event companies book my services explicitly as an ice breaker. So it follows that when the instruments are introduced, I often hit an unusually thick level of ice, the source of which I sometimes cannot assess right away. As a result, I decided to internalize the attitude of being an ice breaker.

I'm convinced that if a service is positioned as an ice breaker to the client, then there is no room for moaning if you hit an icy situation.

Think about it. An ice breaker is built to break ice. If an ice breaker kept roaming in the Indian Ocean, never meeting any icebergs, what would be the whole idea of being an ice breaker at all?

If an ice breaker had a conscious mind and met some ice, then what would it think to itself? It would be glad to come across the ice so that it would have a job to do. The ice breaker would face the ice and break it. This doesn't necessarily mean that the ice breaker needs to break the ice 24/7, because that would wreck its engine in the long run. And it's also not expected for this ice breaker to break every slab of ice on this planet. But if an ice breaker is never breaking any ice, then the whole purpose of being an ice-breaking type of ship is nonsense.

It's actually quite cool to approach people, saying to yourself: "I am an ice breaker." This means that if people react reluctantly to what you're saying, what you're offering or what you're about to provide, you keep calm and think to yourself that this is actually the reason why you're there. You're not there because things are easy. You're there to be yourself and to get through to them. When you don't put too much pressure on yourself, it will be easier for you as well.

The next thing you need to do to foster human connections is to drop the idea of having all the answers. You can't force a connection to happen. Instead, consider yourself to be a facilitator. As a facilitator, you always see the people around you. You make these people grow and you aid them in undergoing personal development. You never focus on yourself and pleasing your ego. Be that kind of facilitator or companion in your communication, knowing that the group already has the wisdom to produce the right answers. That is the right attitude for a facilitator.

Being a facilitator is what all our Drum Cafe event leaders learn to do before they go on duty. This is also what we train the participants in the Drum Cafe Academy trainings to do.

One session places participants in the role of facilitating a complex boomwhacker exercise.

In case you don't remember, boomwhackers are plastic tubes, tuned in six different tones. Since every person can play just one kind of boomwhacker, using these instruments naturally splits the audience into six groups of equal sizes. In the course of using the boomwhacker, we simulate a leadership situation by asking six representatives from each of the six groups to step out and take on the role of the leader of their group. The newly-formed leadership team is asked to gather in front.

You can imagine the situation. There are about 60 people in the room and 10 people get each colour of the boomwhacker set. One representative of each team comes to the centre to be the "manager".

We ask the managers to come up with a groove that they could play with their teams. This is a classic example of a hierarchical situation—a team run by a leader meets to complete a job with their management peers.

A strange but not unusual example of a typical leadership disconnectedness failure happened at a quite exclusive event in Switzerland. Top managers from around the world came together to participate in a top-class workshop to prepare for an upcoming major management position.

If, for example, a major company was going to open up a new branch in India, then the prospective head of that country's operations would come to this special place for a six-week intensive (and expensive) training in order to prepare. We were invited by that institute to run a training for 90 minutes to support the curriculum.

I expected these people to be at a level where they know what is required to make an organisation work and make a group perform. But, interestingly enough, when we asked the six managers to come into the middle, they started putting their heads together and talking about how they could set up the groove for the teams that were sitting around them.

It actually took quite a long time. It was like a strategic meeting of senior leaders thinking about the future of the corporation and how they could make that future great and amazing. During that process, the employees of these six managers were put on hold, waiting for the managers to come up with a groove.

After a while, it got so boring that the team around them started playing without any supervision. One group looked at another and they made a decision about the groove they were going to play. Then, another group joined in too. And while the board leaders were busy in the middle, talking with each other about what they were about to do, there was a rather funky groove actually developing around them.

Suddenly, the managers became silent and they turned around, watching the scene. The head trainer and I were witnessing the situation, curious to see what would happen next. Would they actually realise that there is something developing within the team that they could pick up? That there's competence within their teams that they could incorporate?

They could have just joined their teams and forgotten about their management task because the groove that was already in the air was very cool. But, believe it or not, here is what one manager said:

"Guys, we are working to get a groove together here! Would you please stop playing around? Because it's quite disturbing!"

They truly asked the people to be quiet and wait for the management to come up with the solution. This is a very good example of how ego-driven people often misunderstand their responsibilities in a leadership situation. They could have communicated with their teams. They could have incorporated the teams. They could have asked them if the first team had an idea.

But what they did was to take on the stereotypical role of a leader of the last century. They had to do it. They had to perform. They had the responsibility to make it happen.

The challenge of managing the connections within the leadership team as well as with the people around them completely failed. They had been too busy to see the truth.

The ability to communicate well with human beings depends on the ability to stay connected with *all* the people involved. If you cannot connect with another person for some reason, you cannot perform together.

Another example technically demonstrating this was an event in the so-called "Gasometer," also called the "cathedral of industry culture" in Germany. It is a very unusual event location, rather like a completely empty beer can about 120 meters tall. Standing in the middle of the venue, you experience a five-second reverb tail (the wash of sound that occurs after sound is reflected off a surface in a reverberation). You also hear echoes occurring seven times! And we did a drumming event inside this venue.

The degree of resonance in the Gasometer makes it difficult for people to hear each other even at a normal speech level.

We have a segment in the drumming event where we split the group into two halves, with the left side playing a double stroke and the right side responding to it with another double stroke while the left side pauses. This requires the other side to be able to hear properly. It leads into a left-left, right-right, left-left, right-right sequence.

On almost all occasions, getting this right takes some time; it's a bit shaky and unstable for the first couple of seconds, until the groups automatically synchronize. Like magic, the alternation becomes amazingly stable because the groups start listening to each other very carefully and hear what the other is doing.

It is clear that most of the people attending our trainings and workshops have done many trainings on communication already. But, in most of these cases, listening skills, which include careful listening and active listening, are only taught in a theoretical way. In this exercise, it becomes obvious that if you do not listen carefully and if you do not wait for your slot to step in, then the whole thing becomes shaky and does not work.

It didn't work in the Gasometer at first. The room turned all rhythm into chaos and no one was able to identify whether the sound was coming from the other group or back from the walls.

So we stopped. We quickly reviewed what kind of communication was happening here to make it so difficult. We spoke about the room obviously taking an unusually major role in our drumming. As a result, we decided to bring down the speed of the rhythm and match it to the resonance of that specific room. Instead of playing "against" the room, we played "with" the room, finding out what the response characteristics of the room were, then matching our timing to the room's response. After that, we split the group again and tried to get back to the shared rhythm we had planned earlier.

By doing this, 120 people in the venue achieved perfect resonance. The power and energy of that constant dialogue between the two groups, further amplified by the resonating room, was transformative. If we would've remained in that groove for long, it would've put most of the people present into a trance.

We could have said, "it's not working in this room" and given up. But, with a few adjustments, we turned it into one of the strongest experiences in connecting with everything around us.

The metaphor is quite interesting. You need to set a pace and create a situation where people have a slight chance of connecting with each other in order to communicate properly. It sounds trivial, but it is, in fact, fundamental. If you can't hear, see or feel another person, then how can you possibly respond? If the environment doesn't support proper connectivity, then look for the potential in the environment or change the situation. Connectedness is king in group performance.

It's vital to focus on connectedness.

We did an event for a bank in a combined show with http://www.firedancer.de. This is a group we are familiar with, which performs world-class fire dancing shows all over the planet. Obviously, if you're on stage with a fire dancing group, there's going to be a lot of fire around. It is quite important to have a dedicated briefing session to make sure no one gets hurt by the fire dancing effects shooting out from everywhere.

The sound check, stage positioning and a run-through of the show are actually very important and we take them very seriously.

I arrived early by public rail; the team was coming by car. Unfortunately, the team made a wrong turn while driving to the show and they got diverted and a bit lost.

A fight had started between the driver and the rest of the team and when they finally arrived, they were not only late, but there was also massive tension between the team members.

We were supposed to get straight into the briefing session and sound check. But my team was in a terrible mood, with several members almost shouting at each other.

It is said that a young boy once watched two people standing nose-to-nose, shouting at each other loudly. He thought about why they needed to shout so loudly when they were standing so close. He approached Mahatma Gandhi who responded that we shout at one another when our hearts cannot hear each other.

I put a stop to what we were scheduled to do; we couldn't go on stage while our hearts were disconnected. Instead I did an exercise with my team; it's something that we teach in our trainings as well. It's a good idea to remember what you preach when faced with adversity yourself. But don't think that my musicians, being in bad moods, welcomed that idea at all.

The practice involves sitting in a circle and doing what we call a Knee La Ola. It's a special La Ola wave that you can play on your knee. You can also sit around a table and play it on the table top. This makes it a perfect exercise to do at the beginning of a team meeting.

The rhythm is that of a waltz: one-two-three, one-two-three, one-two-three.

The left hand of the first person plays the first beat. The right hand of the second person plays the second beat. Then the left hand of the third person plays the third beat.

Then we start with the right hand of the first person playing the first beat, the left hand of the second person playing the second beat and the right hand of the second person playing the third beat.

Then the left hand of the second person plays the first beat, the right hand of the second person plays the second beat and the left hand of the next person in the circle plays the third beat. And so on.

With this, you end up with a wobbling groove that moves across a team.

http://tcp-knee-laola.matthias-jackel.com

Because it is rather complex, the idea is not to achieve speed and excellence. It's about linking exactly to the person next to you and seeing when the wave is coming, when you need to take it over and when you have to give it over to the next person.

I asked my team to do that exercise and, as expected, they couldn't do it, even though they were professional percussionists. The reason was not that they couldn't play that groove, because that was, technically, a simple task for them. The reason was that they were not connected. They were in fight mode. But we didn't want to stop playing until everyone had overcome that feeling of being disconnected.

I explained to my team that it was important to calm down and forget about what happened in the car. In order to make that groove work, they needed to see their neighbours and connect with them. If one person had a problem with doing this specific wave, the others needed to link with that person even more, with serenity and compassion, and make it a joyful effort instead of blaming him or her for not performing well.

It is a challenge to aim for these qualities from a starting point full of tension. It took us a full 20 minutes to make this groove work. But after those 20 minutes, we had eliminated that knot of miscommunication and missing connectivity between the team and we turned them into a group again. We helped them to recognise the other people in the group. We connected their body with the groove and we reconnected their hearts to each other, recognising that things only work well when we do them together.

Then we went on stage and did a quick run-through with the time that was left. The show time was about two hours later, and it turned out to be one of the best shows ever. We got three standing ovations during the show, and we all had tears in our eyes when we realised that we had only been able to deliver that kind of performance on stage by becoming a team and by connecting to each other.

The thing that I understood on that day is that connection comes before correction.

If you pause for a second and think about "correcting," you may legitimately argue that there are a lot of things that require improvement all day long. That is very true. Just the last 24 hours have provided me with a long list of things that I think require change. But there's a difference between changing something and someone.

Things can change.

But the attitude of "correcting someone" creates a gap between that individual and you. It leads to blame and isolation and it is usually counterproductive. It never solves the problem. I admit that one of the hardest things is to attempt to connect with a person when you're actually outraged about his or her actions.

But these are the most special moments in life. They give you a chance to grow and new pastures may open up for you. Your whole body tells you to react as usual, but you make the leap and try something different. The more challenging the situation is, the more you need to be connected to yourself in order to make it through.

Even in standard situations, when you meet someone, it makes a huge difference if you start your communication by being connected.

You may try this exercise that you can do easily with another person or in a meeting that you want to start with a connecting element. It is called clapping XY. It's an exercise that originally comes from flamenco music where it creates the basic dance rhythm.

It's done in couples, staying face to face with your partner at a distance of about a meter. Clap normally, moving your hands apart, left and right, and then bringing them together in the centre. Choose a slow and steady tempo. The other person does almost the same thing but moves their hands up and down and then brings them together.

The spot where the hands of the other person meet for clapping is the same spot as yours. So it turns out that you can't clap at the same time because your hands would hit each other's in the centre. Instead, the other will clap while your hands move outwards and vice versa.

If both of you stay at the same speed, this becomes a rhythmic exercise of alternating claps. Keep that stable in the beginning, and then you can try to increase the speed. The only way to do that is by connecting with that person and perfectly synchronising your rhythms.

The fact that both of you are supposed to clap in the same location helps. If you get out of sync, you'll not only hear it but, sooner or later, you'll feel it. Your hands will hit those of your partner, forcing you to restart.

It sounds very simple, but it is an absolutely amazing thing to do when you start a conversation. You will find yourself automatically linking much better with that person. Even when it doesn't work for you in the beginning, keep trying.

Chapter 9 (G#)
Balanced Connections

Albert Einstein said, "Life is like riding a bicycle. To keep your balance, you must keep moving."

It's possible to balance your life via music. Here is a list of ways in which you can make that happen:

- In music, you can take the lead and express yourself. You give a lot to the audience and the other musicians. In this way, you can balance egoism and altruism.
- In music, the structure of the song balances the freedom of the solo. Focus balances out your urge to wander and be free.
- Strength and weakness can be found in the strong and silent notes. Together, these create a musical flow and touch human beings.
- Learning the system eventually allows you to play around with music. This represents the work and play balance in life.

- Music meets you where you are and lets you forget about where you think you should be.
- And finally, you mix harmony and disharmony to create good music. In the same way, you can balance the good and bad in life.

All of that is experienced in music. There are always two sides to every story. And those sides require integration if you want to write the song of life. What you focus on can create a powerful rock song or a sad ballad. It's your choice.

Let me go through this list step by step.

The first thing on the list is the ego; it's one of the strongest influencers holding you back from achieving your potential.

Remember the last chapter. The urge to change "something" that may need changing is different from the urge to change "someone." The latter is an ego-driven projection which clashes with the status quo of the person you want to change. Those projections are built upon experiences and feelings gathered in the past and our idea of what impact that person is going to have on our egocentric future.

The number one reason that we face challenges instead of being neutral and balanced is because we're often unconsciously steered by that force called ego.

There's a lot of literature available about becoming an ego-less person. It's a huge topic and there are books which go deep into it, like the ones by Eckhart Tolle.

I'd like to share some of the experiences I've had about this during our sessions.

How ego-driven a person is vs. how connected that person is becomes obvious in a practice based on the "big bangs" which were introduced earlier. The facilitator puts up his hand and shows the audience the number of strokes by holding up that many fingers. The audience responds by banging on the drums that many times.

In the Drum Cafe Academy training, individuals from the audience take over the role of the facilitator once that exercise is introduced. It is an amazing experience because they may come on stage rather shy and with lots of fears, but they get a massive response in return. What they experience is the buddy sensation of putting a single finger in the air and receiving the breathtaking response of hundreds of drums being struck by people. That's a physical experience where the air is moving so intensely that if you put a hand against a concrete wall, you feel it shaking.

The newly-introduced facilitators certainly enjoy that feeling. It's just too massive, and you can't avoid being carried along by the power of the moment. There's a certain point in time where it becomes obvious whether that person is using this power to give the audience a great time and make them perform together well or whether that person is thinking, "Oh gosh, look how much power I have. Hmmm, what can I possibly do with these people?" Obviously, no one would ever speak that out loud, but it becomes subconsciously apparent to the whole audience when the person starts enjoying the sensation of gaining massive control over such a huge group and then starts using it.

The little difference in the vibe comes from the tendency of the protagonist to either please his ego through mass control or to aim to make it a joyful effort, enjoying the togetherness and connectedness while showing compassion for the mutual achievement of the group. It's a very small difference, but it has a massive effect on the outcome.

Up until now, looking back at the many trainings that we have done, I find that only one out of ten people were able to really focus on the audience, simply because the exercise is so powerful that they fall into the trap of power. It was Abraham Lincoln who said, "Nearly all men can stand adversity, but if you want to test a man's character, give him power."

By doing the "big bang" exercise with participants in our trainings, we actually give the people power and show them the results of their actions. The exercise makes people choose between ego-power and empowerment of the group. We steer the process in such a way that there is no unintentional exposure of any power-hungry characteristics in the protagonist. However, the sequence has the power to unveil the unknown, and, if the mandate is given, we can use it to challenge even those senior groups that think they are doing it perfectly.

It is important to put means in place to become better

aware of the drivers of such dynamics. Babies are not born with the will to power and control. It is something conditioned into them during the socialization process.

The contrast is between egoism and altruism. To start getting more balanced, you need to get an idea of when you are in an ego-focused or maybe even a control and command mode to achieve or gain something and when you are in a mindful and aware mode of connectedness with everything around.

There's a nice story that is said to have happened to the young Buddha and that is also covered in *The Alchemist* by Paulo Coelho. It is the oil spoon story, where the young Buddha is given a spoonful of oil by a king, asking him to walk through his castle while making sure that the oil is not spilled on the floor.

Siddhartha Gautama, the young Buddha, begins to walk through every room of the castle, making sure that not a single drop of oil spills on the floor. He returns with the spoon completely full of oil. But then, the king asks him whether he has seen the paintings in the rooms and whether he could describe them. The young boy can't, of course, because he was so focused on the job of keeping the oil in the spoon.

The king asks him to go again but to make sure that he also looks at all the paintings in the house. This time, the boy comes back to him, aware of all the paintings in the rooms, but the spoon is almost empty because he spilled most of the oil on the floor.

I like this fable a lot because it describes that idea of balance between focus and wandering—the story we have in our minds about a job that needs to be done, a target that must be achieved or a situation that must be avoided on one hand and the open-minded serenity and curiosity to stay connected with everything around, on the other.

You will not get things done without focus, but you will miss important facts if you focus solely on the task. The balance between control and command versus connectedness and the ability to recognize your state of consciousness is vital. There is nothing wrong with being in one state or the other, but it is dangerous to be a "strong boy" or "strong girl" and stick with a must-stay-focused-to-get-it-done habit when you don't have any real need of it or when you don't even recognize it as such.

This leads to the question of being strong or weak and which of these is appropriate at different points of time.

When you don't recognize what you're doing, you don't realise when to let go. I'm sure you know the story of the glass that is filled with water up to the halfway mark and how it can be used to determine a person's worldview and character (you can look at it as half full or half empty).

I like looking at the metaphor from a completely different angle. More than the question of whether it's half full or half empty, it's just a glass of water with a certain weight. No matter how full it is, if you hold it up for a while, that weight will have some effect on you. If you hold that glass up for 15 minutes, you will start to shiver. If you do it for two or three hours, it will hurt a lot. If you do it for two days, you'll kill your shoulder completely.

You can train yourself to become stronger so that you continue to achieve your aim. But you can also choose to see the underlying moral of the story: the water is a weight you carry that you have a choice to drop.

In order to achieve balance and ease in your life, you can put things on the table, free your hand and check if that is something you truly need to keep carrying. This is not a sign of weakness but a sign of strength and wisdom. There is a big difference between the quality of giving up and the quality of knowing when it is enough.

To stay within the metaphor of music, consider the fact that expressive notes can be played in a strong or weak way within a song. It is the mix and balance between both that makes a decent song.

This leads us to the next important item on our list—work-life balance and time management. People talk a lot about this nowadays, and it's an important element when you're attempting to balance your life.

As a matter of fact, time can't be managed.

You can take your time, but you can't *manage* your time.

There is an amazing performance artist by the name of Marina Abramović who made a movie called, *The Artist is Present*. This is a great documentary to watch, and, in the booklet that comes with the DVD, she explains a concept that really changed my mind when it came to work-life balance.

According to Abramović, an artist is always working! An artist is working in their free time, because that's when they get inspired and they're also working when they're sleeping.

Let's say you're a very hard worker for your company and at the end of an exhausting day, you go to sleep. If you call that free time, then you're misunderstanding the situation. You need that sleep in order to remain a hard worker in your workplace.

We tend not to link these things together; we separate them. So we don't understand that spending time with our friends, having hobbies, having a family and balancing our life are actually very important parts of the job itself.

This concept means you are working 164 hours per week! 24x7=164! Everything that you do, at work in your office, as well as the time you spend sleeping, relaxing, talking to co-workers, friends or family, taking care of your kids, reading a book, spending time on your hobby—it's all work! The energy you put into all those actions defines the quality of your work and, since it is all work in one way or the other, it defines the quality of your life.

Everything you do is part of this great thing called life!

This manner of thinking makes you stop believing that you're only a good person if you work 40, 50 or 60 hours in your office. You realise that everything links together. And whatever you do has an outcome. There's a price to pay for everything, so you'd better consider what that price is. Sometimes, that's not easy to foresee, especially when you get into effects that I call long feedback loops.

It's easy to understand the dynamics of long and short feedback loops by looking at sleep time once more.

If you're working on a major project requiring work, day in and day out, to such a point that you don't sleep at all for two nights, then you will find that eventually, your productivity drops almost to zero.

The funny thing is that, in our culture, if you break down and get ill at this point, then people will instantly support you. "Gosh," they'll say, "What you did was not normal. You have to sleep. So better get yourself home and in bed now!"

The reason for this is that sleep is on a very short feedback loop. When you're missing out on sleep, you're doing something with an immediate and crystal-clear result on your physical and mental health. It's an easy-to-see case of cause and effect.

But a lot of things that we do don't have short feedback loops; they have very long feedback loops. It may take weeks or months or even years for these things to have similar effects. And those effects will probably be more severe than sleeplessness.

Things with these long feedback loops might be little things, but they cause you constant pain. You might go along with things, work harder and longer than you should, eat badly, compensate with distractions and drugs and, after a while, you'll wonder why your productivity has gone down. Why are you struggling to cope with the "normal" world around you?

You've no remembrance of where your malaise came from, so you try to explain it with a current situation, not understanding that you've done things with negative effects for so long. You just don't see the long feedback loop between actions and their long-term effects.

What forces us to continue in our negative routines? In our heads, there's a difference between what is and what should be. We think that we must do this and that in order to get somewhere. This causes stress, the effect of which goes deep into your cell structure.

Here is my definition of stress: stress is being here when you want to be there.

That statement isn't only meant to apply to physical space; it's applicable to all types of space. Think of that definition from a holistic perspective of time and space, personal development, abilities, skills, and anything else in which you just are what you are but you think you should be someone else or somewhere else.

Maybe you think you should have learned more in the

past and that's why you're not where you should be. Or maybe you're at work, but you're thinking about your family and you want to be with them instead. Or maybe you are with your family and you think you would rather be working.

All this creates stress. But once you get into the moment, into the here and now, you feel relaxed. All that mind chatter disappears and you have access to all the inspiration and creativity you need to make this a better moment. That is the whole art of recognising and acknowledging the present.

Making music together provides a powerful way to give you a first glance of that state. But you can experience that state from literally anything you do that brings you into the moment. You get into a state of flow and you lose track of time and space.

The fundamental first step is to become aware of the beautiful balance between harmony and disharmony. This balance depends on your decisions about what to do in your life and how to do it. It is best achieved by taking radical responsibility for your actions.

I once had a lady from a big bank in a workshop who told me that her life would be much more in harmony if she were shown some respect by her colleagues. She was working at the front desk of a bank. She would say, "Good morning" to everyone, but she just hated the way people passed by without responding. This daily feeling of not being respected and other issues in the company even led her to consider suicide.

We had a serious talk about what kind of influence she actually has. While she wanted to be respected and be compensated for her actions, I suggested that she might also consider what those people were going through. They may not have intended to disrespect her while passing by. Maybe they were just not able to respond with a "Good morning" at that very moment. There was no reason for her to take it personally.

In fact, there might have been a good reason why they didn't respond. Maybe they were having a bad morning, or they were thinking about their jobs. Or maybe some other serious topic was on their mind. If she was only saying "good morning" to get a "good morning" in return, she was making herself a victim of circumstances and a victim of the reactions of those people.

It would be much more constructive if she made the decision "just to give" to those people, no matter how they responded. That would be more likely to plant a seed in the heads of those people. If she avoided judging the situation, stopped expecting something in return and remained in a giving mode, then maybe someday, those people would return and say "Good morning" as well. Or even if they didn't say it, she would still have given them a nicer morning by wishing them when they didn't seem to be in a very good mood.

When you step out of a situation where you consider yourself to be the victim of something, you can balance the power of your emotions and replace it by feeling the moment and understanding that, at every point in your life, you have 100% control of how you react to something. You can decide what you give. And if you give, you will always have the ability to control the situation instead of waiting for others to do it. Whether or not your life is balanced depends on the effort you put into balancing it.

Let me repeat this because it's an important point: unconditional giving makes you a leader in that situation. If you have expectations instead, you make yourself dependent upon others.

Leading or depending. Everything you do and the way you look at your world falls into one of these two categories. One workshop I provide helps people in setting the right focus.

Instead of drums, we can run the interactive event just with drumsticks as well. The instruments we're using are 100% wooden drumsticks with no varnish. In the drumsticks ritual, we hand out pencils and spend some time writing down one side of the story on one drumstick.

For example, people might write about areas where they see hindrances or problems. They may write about the reasons why they're not able to develop further in their lives. They may write about the things that make them dependent on others.

Once done, we spend time on every single note made on that first drumstick to find its positive equivalent and note it on the other drumstick. Which means that for everything a participant considers a hindrance, they take the time to figure out what the alternatives are, where a decision can be made and how they can take responsibility for themselves and their lives by turning that thing around, reshaping it and reframing it into something resourceful and helpful. Then we take both drumsticks and make music with them again.

Trying to clap with one hand is impossible. We need to have both drumsticks in order to make music together. If you focus only on the negative things in your life, it is like clapping with one hand. If you focus on only the positives, then it is the same thing. You will not have sound in your life. It's only if you look at both and integrate them, accept them, acknowledge them and appreciate them that you will be able to progress.

In the next step, if that is required, after appreciating and seeing both sides of the story, we can proceed towards what we would like to focus on in the future. We do that by taking the positive drumsticks and storing them safely. We take the other one to a fireplace. We put the drumsticks with the bad thoughts into the fire and we verbalize what this is about. We talk about letting go and we talk about the decisions that we have to make in life in order to keep the balance. Then we light the fire and burn those drumsticks together. If requested, we can even keep the ashes at the end and use them in the future. For example, they can be used as fertilizer to plant a flower. In this way, all negative things can grow into something positive.

No matter what we look at, we always have the choice to focus on problems or focus on the resources that can bring all of us forward.

Gandhi said, "Life is not a problem to solve, but a mystery to live."

Chapter 10 (A)
Connect Yourself

It's getting personal now. How can you connect with yourself then? The universal answer seems to be: by being conscious and mindful. The magic wand to achieve connection with yourself is contemplative practice. The challenge lies in the word "practice" and the fact that we don't stick with practicing. Or we often practice the wrong thing.

I first had to understand what practice is. The idea that practice leads to championship is nonsense. Practice *is* championship. You should never practice to reach a goal or learn an art. Practicing is the goal and the art by itself. When I did a recap of my practice during my years running Drum Cafe, I realised that I changed myself without even recognising that I'm doing it.

Basically, my original nature at 35 was that of a very cognitive thinker. I was a rigid, performance-oriented perfectionist. With those qualities in my bag, I founded Drum Cafe Germany. That was positive and helpful because it enabled me to build a highly professional company delivering top-quality services, all the way from first client contact to contracts and operations.

But when I got on stage, I concentrated on connecting with the audience. In the beginning, I wasn't aware of what that meant to me. But even at times when business was booming, I brought my cognitive engine down to nil almost every other day when I was on stage.

It was an unexpectedly intensive way of meditating every time I ran an event. When I got off stage, I was relaxed, balanced and feeling at ease. It was not about the performance or the thrill of the standing ovations. That was not the point for me. The point was the peace that was happening inside of me. If I felt ill shortly prior to the event, then I felt healthy afterwards. If I felt pressure on my shoulders before, then I felt relief afterwards.

It took me several years to realise that the sheer number of events that I did constituted a contemplative practice without even thinking about it. All this talking about not thinking and preventing mind chatter was a theoretical thing to me in those days. I didn't even intend to try it or become spiritual in any way. It was a strange situation and I only understood it in hindsight.

It was around 2012, after eight years of Drum Cafe, that I first experienced a very unusual kind of amnesia at an event. We'd done 40 minutes of a show in Frankfurt, Germany, and I got to the point where I introduced my team. They were all friends of mine from day one of starting the business. And I was playing a groove, ready to start talking when I realised that I couldn't remember the name of my lead drummer.

It was quite a funny situation because, while I was introducing the other names to applause, I stretched over to him and whispered into his ear, "Hey, what's your name again?"

He gave me a strange look, continued drumming and said, "Are you f... kidding me?"

I said, "No, I truthfully can't remember. What's your name?"

"I'm Michail!" he said.

"Ah, yes, thank you."

I turned around to the audience and introduced Michail.

On that day, I accepted this occurrence with a little nervous smile. But over time, it started happening more frequently and I was concerned that it might be a medical problem. Then I realised that, rather than being a brain issue, it was just the effect of something very positive that had happened to me. Over the years, I was able to get so much into the here and now and connect with the people in the room that every cognitive overhead decreased.

Remembering names is part of a cognitive effort and, while I was doing my "stage meditation," those areas of my brain went into "pause" mode. I realised that this is not a problem but rather a sign of the depth of my connection and mindlessness in the course of such an event.

Once I realised that fact, I was able to integrate it, making sure that I kept enough of my brain present for the things that I needed to know cognitively for doing the event. These included the short briefing from the client and the names of my people. I realised that if I put too much effort into keeping facts present during the event, it prevented me from deepening the connection. So I also learned to outsource brainwork to stickers and little notes in the corner of a flipchart, in case cognitive effort was required by the nature of the actual event.

If I have a complex briefing to remember, I can still focus on the core of the experience i.e., connecting with the moment. I have the ability to switch off everything else. When I'm on stage, the normal world around me vanishes. I'm completely in the moment. There is just the audience, the room, the musicians and me. Always. To me, that is the power of practice.

I had times in my life when I tried to do some "proper" meditating. I also tried yoga methods, but they didn't really work for me. I never had the patience. I completely misunderstood meditation as an exercise in addition to my daily routines.

I first had to realise that I can meditate in every single moment. I can meditate while I'm cooking. I can meditate while I'm driving. Meditation is simply the ability to transfer my experience from stage to every moment and connect with where I am and what I'm doing. During meditation, I have no thoughts about what brought me there or where I'm going to go afterwards. I replaced mechanical actions while my mind was wandering into presence of mind while performing any and all actions.

Connecting with yourself requires doing things that support your development and that you keep doing because you enjoy doing them. They help you to reconnect with the moment and diminish isolation. They break through the bubble of your mind and help you to regain access to yourself and the now.

A firecracker on New Year's eve is a great metaphor to show you what I mean by "bubble." When you take the black powder out of the firecracker, put it on a table and light it, then you will only see a short flash of sparkling light. When you leave the same black powder in the paper wrapping, it creates an explosion. The more of the black powder you have and the more you lock it in a sealed box, the better the cracker will work.

That black powder exists everywhere in our day-to-day lives. It consists of all the small and big things that you think of as "bad" experiences and keep gathering throughout your life. If you go through life collecting these experiences in your memories and your soul, wrapping them around you in many layers all the time, then one day, you might become a bomb.

The question is: how many layers do you put around yourself before you see that the alternative is to open yourself up? Because if you take a little cracker, break it up in the middle and then light it, then that cracker becomes harmless; it just turns into a little flashing light. By opening it up and dismantling the layers, you free that energy and make it into a light instead of a big bang.

You need to take off these layers and let people look inside you. You need to share your thoughts and feelings instead of becoming a dangerous emotional bomb in the course of your life.

In our trainings, I often hear that even just the idea of making music scares people off. The fear of making music is often just the fear of opening up, because people can look into your soul. It is a very fundamental question of life: do you want to open up or do you want to remain closed?

Actively reconnecting with your past is a great start and there are many useful tools to help you to do that. One is a timeline of your past. It comes from classic psychology and is something which does not require much guidance. So you can easily do it yourself. You will probably understand the concept rather quickly, but please reserve a minimum of two or three hours to get it done.

Take at least two or three flip-chart-sized pieces of paper and glue them together lengthwise to create a long rectangular paper roll. Place it horizontally on the longest table you can find. Then draw a solid line in the middle of your roll, from left to right. The left end of the roll should have your date of birth. The right end indicates today. Then go through the roll and put marks on it for every ten years.

Start with the big events in your life. Mark the first one that comes to mind at the right position in your timeline. Take another colour and make a drawing illustrating the event, and describe it in a few words. Don't make your description too long and detailed; just a sentence or two will be enough.

The most important thing to do is to position the event more towards the top of the paper roll when you remember it positively. Sad or bad memories go more towards the bottom. Neutral experiences are drawn right at the line in the middle.

Start with the big events and move on. Take your time. Dig deeper and look for the positive and the negative. Use as many colours as you can. Make it a work of art. Take a full day to do it if you can. It is an important job to do.

Look at your life positively, and show it to your partner and the people you trust. You may say that others don't open up to you; so why should you open up to them? You may also argue that it's best to let the past rest. My only response to that is that you need to be the pioneer when it comes to opening up. You can set the pace and lead others. Hence, let me share with you the timeline I made in 2014. I have even used different colours for different areas of my life, dividing it into "Personal," "Relationships" and "Business" sections. You can't see that in this single colour copy, but it may give you an impression of how a timeline should look.

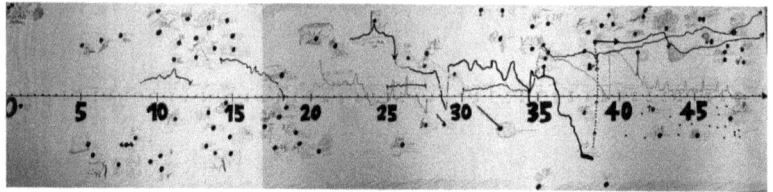

Many people are afraid of facing their own past and sharing it. The only thing you have to do is integrate your past instead of hiding it. At least don't hide from yourself. Approach your past with a positive outlook; don't consider it a problem. It led you to where you are today and it added strength to you as a person. So let go of your negativity.

You may stop reading here and just give it a go.

* * *

Then moving forward to the now, we need a way to stay connected with ourselves and our surroundings. We need to avoid going into a bubble due to old patterns of thought and destructive emotions like fear.

A good way of keeping ourselves in balance is by introducing the "barometer of connectedness." I like the word "barometer" for this idea because it is linked to the "highs" and "lows" in the weather. Fog, limited visibility, clouds, the cold and even the rain are all "lows." The warmth, the sun, brightness, health and spectacular views are all "highs." The weather is a perfect metaphor for highs and lows in the climate of your relationships.

Your "barometer of connectedness" should resemble the speed display of your car. While you're driving, you look at the display to check your speed. You always have that in front of you. If you just got your driver's license and you're not a very experienced driver, then you may look at that display rather often. But after a while, when you've become more experienced, you don't look at that display so much anymore. You have it in front of you, you recognise it, you know where the numbers are and that helps you steer through cities and streets without speeding.

You can do the same when you interact with a person. Just imagine a little display like a barometer that goes from 0 to 10. 0 stands for being completely disconnected and 10 stands for being completely connected to the person in front of you. Sure, that is a subjective assessment, but assessing it means recognising it. While you're talking, you just take a short moment to look at that barometer in your mind and see what it says.

If the barometer is not closer to 10 than to 0, if there is no connectedness, then you can actively work against it. By making that an exercise while you're having conversations, you come to realise that most of the challenges you experience in your communication arise because you separated from that person i.e., you were not connected anymore. Even a fight can be had in a more constructive manner if you consciously make a decision about your level of connectedness. There is a great difference between interacting with another person in a conscious way and interacting in an automatic way, without thinking about it. The barometer simultaneously shows you how much you connect yourself to old and destructive emotions (making you disconnect to the other person) or with real-time feelings in the here and now (making you connect with the moment and the person in front of you).

If the "barometer of connectedness" is a meter that moves from left to right, then the "scale of words" is a meter that is positioned forward and backwards between the other person and you. It is the second means I've developed to balance while being in contact with others. Think of a classic scale with bowls on each side and a needle in the middle, moving towards the side of the bowl with more weight.

Imagine that scale standing in-between you and the person you're talking to. One of the bowls is on your side and one is on the side of the other person. If you put weight into your bowl, then the needle turns towards you. The weight comes from the words that you choose.

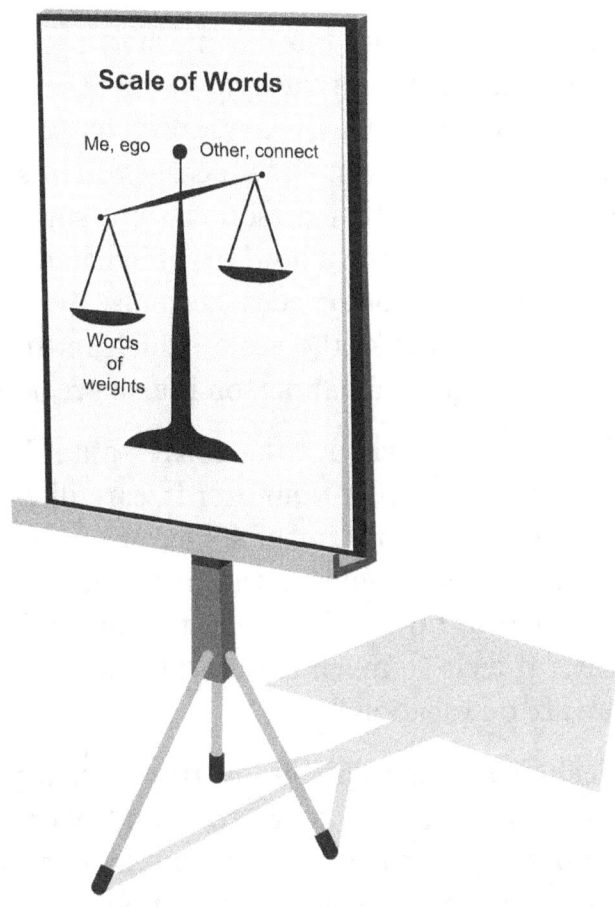

Self-righteous, toxic and emotional words of the past, as well as words that are blaming, arguing, doubting and looking for revenge, have strong meaning; they are heavy in terms of weight. They are driven by fear and come straight from the ego.

Healing words of acknowledgement, words that bring you to the moment, self-revealing words as well as words that express feelings, trust, openness and connectedness are light. They are driven by love and come straight from the heart.

The position and movement of the needle shows where the focus and the dynamics of the conversation are. If you add many heavy words on your side, then the other person can either accept you by serving your ego and fear or that person can put similar words of weight into their own bowl to get in balance. That way, the weight on both sides becomes more and more and finally breaks the scale, which means that your relationship with that person is also breaking down.

If you want to change the conversation in a positive way, then consider your words carefully. I give you a simple example. Imagine you are on vacation and your partner is holding you in his or her arms. This moment in time feels special to you. And maybe you say, "It feels so much better to be in your arms when we are on vacation."

Technically, that might be true. Since you are on vacation, you have more time and energy to spend with your partner. But if you look at the words carefully, you'll see that they contain both, a positive message and a comparison to what you usually have with your partner. In a way, you are setting a standard for how you should feel in the future while embracing your partner. And this comes across as a judgement. It is a mix of lovely words that come from the heart and words that come from the ego which was not pleased in the past. The ego is insisting that it wants to be treated better in the future.

That makes the needle of the scale move towards you, indicating that the conversation is more about you and not your partner. If you had just said, "It feels great lying in your arms," your words would have been light and easy. They would have only imparted the positive message of the moment. And, even though you had not said anything, the other person would keep that feeling in mind for future reference without feeling bad about how a simple embrace did not live up to your standards in the past.

Even when you feel that the needle is moving towards the other person because what you hear drives you crazy and makes you disconnect, you have a chance to look at which of your own buttons have been pushed that led you to that reaction. And you can decide how you want to move on in that situation.

You can see the needle moving and it is up to you to decide how you interpret it. You can avoid further movement towards the other by pleasing your ego and adding heavy words or, alternatively, you can consider to what extent your ego is interpreting the words coming from the other side to make the scale only appear as though it's moving away from you.

It is a matter of radical self-responsibility to start with yourself when you see the scale moving in either direction.

Both instruments will help you reassess your actions and give you a chance to steer in a positive direction. But, most importantly, you will soon see that when you get in trouble, it's because you've been unaware of the scale and the barometer. Just recall them and approach that person one more time, giving it another try with these little techniques in mind.

It all boils down to whether you want to be right or whether you want to be happy. If you insist on being right, then connectedness and happiness are mostly left out. If you are connected with yourself, you don't need to be right in the eye of any external entity. Inner peace, inner joy and love come from being connected with yourself. And you get connected with yourself whenever you disconnect your mind and reconnect with your body and your heart.

A very simple way to do this (and also the one you hear about the most) is focusing on your breath. Inhale through your nose so that you feel it deep in your abdomen. Then exhale from your mouth and watch the air flow through your body. Hundreds of books reference this practice and I don't feel like it's necessary for me to add anything more. Therefore, I'd like to show you a method that will help you to get a bodily sensation while keeping your mind busy and away from too much thinking.

Since this method is about connecting with your heart, sit on a comfortable chair or lay down on the floor. With your right hand, take your left wrist and search for your pulse. Once you've found it, listen to it.

There is a certain variability in your heartbeat, so that pulse keeps changing. It gets faster when you inhale and it slows down slightly when you exhale. The variability is more in babies and you can hear this during pregnancy when you do an ultrasound. It gets reduced over the years until it's not really recognizable anymore when you're an adult.

So when you listen to your heartbeat, you tune in to your heart. Sing a rhythmic tune to the beat of your heart, silently or loudly. Or pick a dance of your choice, like a waltz, and imagine dancing to the beat of your heart. Since the beat keeps changing a little bit, you constantly need to reconnect to it. This is a great daily practice for reconnecting with yourself.

While you are listening to your heart, think about one more thing. I recently read an article which told me that a typical human heart beats 6 billion times in a 75-year lifespan. I was trying to wrap my head around that huge number and make it tangible. I thought about what else we have on the earth which also numbers 6 billion. And then, I realised that this number is very close to the number of human beings living on earth. The number was 7,595,500,883 at the time when I checked it on the Internet. It is not uncommon to get to the age of 95, is it? That means that a person getting to the age of 95 owns a heart that has the power and endurance to beat once for every single human being on this planet. Isn't that amazing?

At the same time, your heart needs only about 20 seconds to beat for that little group of people which owns half of the fortune of this entire planet.

However, if your brain is going berserk at high speed, you may need a tool that is a bit stronger. It has the same effect as a bit of stretching when you get very stiff. I call it ZIP code drumming.

You can connect with yourself and the moment with a simple rhythmic exercise. Everyone can do it easily, no matter where they are. The name of the exercise comes from the idea that, after learning the system, you can start drumming the postal code of the area you live in on your body. For that, the numbers 0-9 are assigned a sequence of claps across your body.

0 is indicated by a pause.

1 is indicated by a clap of your hands.

2 is indicated by a clap and lightly hitting your right shoulder.

3 is indicated by a clap, lightly hitting your right shoulder with your right hand and then lightly hitting your left shoulder with your left hand.

4 is indicated by a clap, lightly hitting your left shoulder, lightly hitting your right shoulder and then lightly hitting your right hip with your right hand.

This goes all the way up to 9, which is indicated by a clap, lightly hitting your right shoulder, your left shoulder, your right hip, your left hip, your right butt, your left butt, a step with your right foot and one with your left foot.

For a 9, you follow these 9 steps all the way through. But you can also combine them. That means that if you take your own postal code, you can start with the first number, follow the sequence that indicates that and then, without a pause, do the next number and so on. Once you have finished with the last number of that postal code, you jump back to the start.

Assume that your ZIP code is 1212. That would be indicated by this sequence: clap, clap, right shoulder, clap, clap, right shoulder, and so on...

Once you have internalised that method, you can literally take any string of numbers and do a body percussion while reading them.

Whenever you need to switch off your brain, just look for the next string of numbers you see and clap them out for a minute or so.

I understand that this exercise seems childish. Clapping around on your body? What kind of effect could that have? But we have to distinguish between being childish and childlike. It is very important to remain childlike and do things that help us to develop as human beings. Like Steve Jobs once said, "Stay hungry, stay foolish."

With this simple postal or ZIP code exercise, you keep

your brain busy and away from destructive thinking. You activate your whole body and all four extremities. You get moving and experience a bodily sensation. You activate the left and right side of your brain simultaneously. You also activate unused areas of your brain and connect brain areas that don't usually work together.

In actual fact, your whole brain would shine like a Christmas tree if you saw it in a computer resonance scan. The areas of your brain that start working due to the left-hand and right-hand movements usually work only when you're dreaming. At this point, there is massive activity going on in your brain, but none of it is what we consider "thinking." You are improving your life by using your mind in a richer way than you do during normal cognitive work.

Mindlessness doesn't mean being brain-dead. Your mind is still being used but in a different way.

Just get it started. Get into the practice. Get moving, get better and get active. Learning can be done by playing. Play with every moment and try to reshape it. Every moment holds the opportunity for a contemplative practice.

As a final example, I'd like to pick up from the hearing exercise in Chapter 7 (F#): the emotions that came up when the phone was ringing.

Next time your phone is ringing, don't pick it up right away.

At the 1st ring, take a deep breath.

At the 2nd ring, be grateful for one thing this day has already given you.

At the 3rd ring, pick up the phone.

If the caller is gone by that time, that call wasn't important anyway. But with that practice, you'll approach the person calling quite differently than you would when you automatically pick up the phone.

You can make that a new habit and you can change any habit you want. Remember that you need 8-12 weeks to change a habit. You can start right here and right now, using a form of meditation created to help you get into contact with yourself and activate that inner being that helps you connect with people without involving your ego, like you usually do.

You can do this meditation every time before interacting with a group of people. It doesn't matter if the interaction is a presentation, a performance, a conversation, a workshop or a training.

This is an additional service to you as a reader of the book, that is provided in writing as well as in the form of an audio file.

http://tcp-meditation.matthias-jackel.com

* * *

Sit down or lie on the floor in a position that feels good to you. Keep your arms close to your body. Or if you're seated, you can put them on your upper thighs. We'll use a short body scan to bring you into a state of relaxation.

Take a deep breath. Inhale and exhale.

With the next exhale, close your eyes and look at a point on the floor or on the wall in front of you. Then slowly relax.

As soon as you notice that your thoughts have started travelling, just recognise them and bring your consciousness back to the part of your body that you're currently focusing on.

Start with your feet. Feel the spot at which your feet touch the ground or the floor and notice your heels, your toes and your instep carefully.

Then focus on your lower leg. Then move from the lower leg to the calves and the shin bone.

Now wander with your consciousness to the knees and the upper thighs. Feel how the upper thighs are positioned on the floor or on the chair that you're sitting on.

Move on and concentrate on your belly.

Inhale deeply into your belly and feel how your abdomen goes up. Then feel how it goes down while you exhale.

Feel how your back lies on the floor or against the

chair back. Are the muscles in the lower part of your back relaxed? Just check if your shoulders are relaxed, instead of hunching up.

Then relax each and every muscle in your face as well. Check if your jaw is locked or relaxed. Or if the eyelids are closed in a relaxed way.

Feel your arms. Recognise the point at which your arms meet the surface they are lying on and feel your upper arms, elbows, lower arms and fingers.

Due to that feeling of deep relaxation and that consciousness of your body, you might have some epiphanies. You might discover some deeper truths in your coming performance.

Just imagine yourself on stage or in front of people. The audience is in front of you. You look directly into the eyes of the people who are looking at you. Your feet are deeply connected with the floor. You feel that connection with the ground. It's a connection that feels long-lasting. Strong roots go into the floor, reach every person in the room and touch them.

You are connected with every person in the room in a unique, wonderful, way.

Across this connectedness, you send energy to the audience. That is what the participants feel on a deeper level. Your performance, your looks, your pain, your thoughts and your voice are all elements that matter.

We have been trained to recognize things which are on the surface. But beyond these superficial things, there's music, and it is able to create a connection between people across all borders.

Music is the only way to look into the soul of a person directly. You can activate the *melicus* i.e., the "musician inside of you." In order to do that, just open up your soul to the people in front of you and feel how they accept this present.

This connectedness is independent of how people look at you. It is just connectedness. It's the feeling that everything is the way it is and that everything is okay the way it is. Someone is looking at you and you see doubt in his face. Maybe you feel a thick element of ice at the moment that you get into the room. Maybe.

But keep in mind that you can never know what the muscles in the face of a person are really doing. You don't know what thoughts are truly in the room.

That is the task of an ice breaker. The ice breaker doesn't get nervous when it hits ice. That's what it was built for. How boring would it be for an ice breaker if it was just another ship in the Caribbean Sea?

The ice and the ice breaker both have their purpose. Both have a right to exist. The moment when they come together, they connect in a magical, cosmic way.

Just think about it. Who said that we are only good when we do something extraordinary?

Those are stories that we're telling ourselves. They are the means we use to define our value.

But beyond these values, there's a deeper truth. This

truth is that, deep inside, people do not want to look up at your performance. Instead, they just want to be accepted as human beings and loved exactly as they are.

Whether they think you're a genius or they find you creepy, they are allowed to be the way they are in their enthusiasm for what you do. Similarly, they're allowed to be the victims of their doubts and fears; no one is going to judge them for these.

That is a powerful message that you are sending. Maybe it doesn't reach everyone in the first place. Sometimes, it requires patience and trust to make sure that a message reaches the people. Maybe they get it only subconsciously, but they do get it.

Feel the energy that is flowing between you and the rhythm, the dialogue and the stimulus of the moment. If someone is saying something to you and you start a dialogue, then that is jazz i.e., verbal improvisation. The beauty in the melody of this dialogue becomes obvious if we accept the harmony in the same way as we're willing to accept the disharmony.

Like life, music can only work with the game of harmony and dissonance.

With that change from tension to relaxation, in such a field of connectedness, you have nothing left to gain.

You make a contribution simply by being present.

Everything else comes on its own. Out of this consciousness about the things around you, you draw your inner peace, your love and your joy.

Get out to the people and connect. For that, you only need to stay with the people. Enjoy the feeling. Everything is good. You are good the way you are. You are a present to this world and you are a present to the people that you're going to speak to now.

With the next exhale, you open up your eyes. Take some deep breaths, stretch and straighten yourself. Then go out onto your stage.

Chapter 11 (A#)
Counter-Connections

How does the butterfly emerge from the caterpillar? I'm going to answer that question at the end of this chapter because, here, I would like to address an important point in the process of practicing the things that I've outlined so far. When you start talking to people, especially business people, about peace, joy, love, connectedness and spirituality, they're not necessarily going to welcome you with open arms.

A good friend of mine is a very high-level person at a telecommunications company. He knows me for decades and witnessed the development of the program along with my own personal development. We had ongoing conversations about how that idea matches the way business is run these days.

One day, he stared right into my eyes and said, "Matthias, you're truly trying to turn a big wheel here, and I don't know if the companies are ready for that."

I'm convinced that the world is ready for it. And the companies would do well to consider it, too. I noticed myself that there are a couple of reasons why people work against change. For the typical five motivations that I came across, I'm going to tell you a story that will help you to shift your mindset. I'm going to help you to look at things differently so that you can deal with them. It is important to know how to do this when you move on to the last chapter which is about becoming a connectedness ambassador.

I start with number one, which is old mindsets and patterns of thought.

We were invited to attend a series of eight workshops with the employees of a bank that was undergoing some serious changes. They had planned to do a fishbowl where people could bring up items with the board members.

We did the congruent communication flip chart experiment that was mentioned in chapter 4. Our job was to give the people a stretching and warm up so that they would take the chance and really speak out their thoughts later in the fishbowl.

What happened at the first three sessions was that, after that stretching, people truly came up with good questions of a serious nature. But these questions were not really welcomed by the board members. These weren't the questions that the board members expected. And their reaction was to wonder why the employees were bringing up those things instead of just facing the challenge and taking action.

So the first three sessions became more of a fight

between the leaders and the employees about who was right and who was wrong. Arriving at the venue to run the fourth session, I expected that the leaders would cancel my contribution simply because they wanted the employees to stop moaning and deliver. I was suspicious that what we were adding to the process may just open up a conversation that was actually not welcome.

It was unclear whether the board members would understand the point of view of their employees or whether they would go with their current mindset and tell us, "We understand that you open people up to speak their minds, but this is actually not what we really want."

The lady who was leading the board welcomed me that day in a very friendly manner. So I actually thought to myself, "Well, maybe something different will happen today."

We did the flip chart experiment and spoke about congruent communication just as we had done before. People went into the fishbowl, openly and honestly. Some direct, concrete and valid but very tough questions came up.

After hearing some questions, the board member I had spoken to before became rather silent and she spoke to the employees, saying, "You know, for a long time in my career, I have been told that telling the employees too much of the truth is not a good strategy, because they can simply not digest it. Now, I have realised that this is probably the wrong strategy. This is the strategy we have always followed, but I don't like it either. I think that the only way of going through this difficult time is if we do it together and if we are open to each other. We need to accept the other's concerns and speak honestly and openly about them.'

The fishbowl that followed was completely different than the ones that came before. It was filled with openness and detail. It was filled with depth and acknowledgement. It was filled with human beings working with each other and talking about the things that have to be worked out. It was a palpable kind of love.

One employee commented to the board at the end: "The facts you told us may not be pleasant. But the way you said them, the honesty in your words and the way you treated us: all these things give me confidence. Now I know that I'm at the right company and that the best thing to do is to stay here and deal with our challenges, together with you."

When we drop the roles and masks created by conditioning, things can become passionate.

Second reason why people work against change is because of simple misunderstandings.

A while ago, I did an event for a huge telecommunications company. It was running smoothly. But while I was right in the middle of doing the big bangs exercise with 2,000 participants in front of me, a lady came on stage, approached me and whispered in my ear that I should go offstage.

I continued making signs with my fingers and doing the big bangs exercise. I simultaneously turned around to her to say, "No, I'm sorry I cannot go right away! Give me five minutes and I'll bring this to a proper end and then I'll go offstage."

She said, "No, no. You need to stop immediately, and you need to go offstage *now*!"

I turned back to her with my hand in the air. I was working with 2,000 people in front of me. I asked, "Do we have any serious issue? Do we have a fire alarm or something like that?"

She said, "No, I just need you to get offstage."

I looked at her and I said clearly, "I'm not going offstage now because I have 2,000 people in front of me. And if you don't give me a good reason, then I just want to make sure that the experience that they're going through is a round and solid one which is brought to a proper end. I'm happy to go offstage in five minutes."

She said, "Are you going to take responsibility for that?"

And I said, "Yes, for sure. I am going to take responsibility for that."

You need to understand that all this happened while I was doing stops and gos, two strokes and three strokes. I was indicating this to the audience with one hand and speaking to the lady simultaneously, trying to make sure that no one in the audience realised that we were currently having an argument.

I brought this event to a good end after a little more than five minutes. Luckily, we had been close to finishing anyway. The event manager approached me later, and she was really happy about the result. She loved it and gave me a lot of positive feedback.

Then I asked her what had happened. Why did that lady come up and ask me to go offstage?

She responded that she'd seen it happen, but she had no clue why.

Later, it turned out that the lady who approached me was an assistant who picked up a panicked call from catering which said that the dessert was going to melt if they didn't serve it right then. But it wasn't as though we had been late. The catering department had prepared the dessert too early.

If I had followed that rigid call from the lady and left the stage without any reason, I would not have performed the task assigned to me by my client. I would have, most likely, jeopardized my reputation as an entertainer and trainer on stage in front of 2,000 people.

I had a long conversation with that lady afterwards. She was in tears since she had blindly followed the instructions of the catering company. It was a complete misunderstanding.

If you're getting arguments against what you do, have a non-emotional conversation to understand the reason behind it, and if it doesn't convince you, then stick with your strategy.

A third reason why people work against change is because they get competitive.

You may have heard that the only way to motivate people is by putting them into competition and judging the results. But judgement is never the right way. It's a mind-driven act of separation and most contemplative practice aims to diminish it. There's a very nice metaphor in music that you can consider to rethink competition.

We still live in a world where some huge IT and computer companies believe they can gain a better market position by making life difficult for those who are not evangelists of their products. They do this by refusing to open up interfaces and making their programs incompatible with those of other companies.

It is never to the benefit of the client when you make their life more complex instead of easy, which should be the aim of an IT and computer company.

Let's transfer that situation into music. Think about Peter Gabriel and Phil Collins, who used to play in the same band, Genesis, a while ago. Both moved on to very successful solo careers and both of them had concerts around the world.

If they thought like IT companies, they would never bring each other on stage again. Phil Collins would be afraid that if Peter Gabriel was featured in his concert, and if he sang better than Collins did on that day, then people would buy Gabriel's CD and not Collins'. But that is not how people think in a live music concert.

Instead, Phil Collins features Peter Gabriel in his own concert just to give the whole experience a boost. He wants to make the concert even better. And his technique makes the concert so great that people forget about money and just buy the CDs of both singers.

That's what you need to do instead of always thinking in terms of competition. By integrating all solutions available and giving more value to the people, you are enabling clients to spend even more than before.

Let go of the idea of developing your business by making your competitors look bad. Instead, start looking for the best experience for your clients. It will completely change your business and your world, in general.

The fourth reason why people resist change is because of outdated and ridiculous rules.

Rules are instituted to make society work. But the one thing I would like you to consider when someone is telling you that something is against a rule, is the mantra-like power of constantly following old and stupid rules.

I'm German, and we have a reputation for setting strong rules. And we are probably the only ones in the world who stand at the traffic light, afraid to cross the road at two o'clock in the morning, when there are no cars passing by. Still, we're patiently waiting for the light to turn green.

By nature, Germans have a tendency to stick with the rules and that positions me well to make you reconsider the rules yourself.

Often, people set bizarre and crazy rules for purely opportunistic reasons. You can see this in the following example.

In Germany, you are not free to design the struts of a staircase even in private houses. It is not allowed because, if the struts are built longitudinally, then kids might climb up and have an accident. The motivation behind the rule is safety, which is fair enough.

It's funny that we are not talking about a recommendation but a construction law. It's plain forbidden to design your struts in a different way.

Still, in the same country, we have country roads with cars passing by in both directions at a relative speed of 200 km/h. How safe is that? But we accept it because we grew up with it and we are not given an alternative except to avoid those streets. Highways have separate lanes in both directions, but other streets, including streets in residential areas, cannot be separated for economic reasons. So, we leave them the way they are. If cars crash into each other because someone was looking at their mobile or had fallen asleep, we blame the motorist but not the system.

Similarly, in Germany, we are obliged to put on our seatbelts in our cars. This is how it's done in many other places in the world. The motivation is safety and there is no question that it makes life safer when you wear a seatbelt.

But have you ever thought about the motorbike passing by with a father and his 10-year-old kid behind him, who is only holding on to the handholds or daddy's belly at 100 km/h? We are willing to accept literally every dangerous action if the majority of the public can take advantage of it and if a lobby is strong enough to push it through.

But even if a rule made sense at a certain time, it may later become outdated. It's just that no one notices when this happens because they've gotten so used to following that rule.

Let me stick with the example of public transport and give you something interesting to think about. In Germany, we have to keep a certain distance between us and the car in front of us. And that number, in meters, is supposed to be half of the number of the speed of your car, which is in kilometers. So if you're driving at 100 km/h, you have to have a 50-meter space between you and the car in front of you or you get a ticket if captured on camera.

This rule was introduced to compensate for reaction time when something happened in front of you. It was basically a great idea that worked well when there was less traffic. But let me show you a little bit of math that I did while I was stuck in a traffic jam.

If you keep that distance between you and the next

car, then it actually doesn't matter how fast you are going. There's still a maximum number of 2,000 cars that can pass through one lane in one hour. Let me explain that. Take a very long row of cars, all driving at a constant speed of 100 km/h, keeping a perfect distance of 50 meters between themselves and the car in front, according to the rule. If you stand on the street and look at these cars passing by for exactly one hour, then you will realise that exactly 2,000 cars have passed by.

Car number one passes by. Car number two is 50 meters behind. At a speed of 100 km/h, car number two needs 1.8 seconds to cover those 50 meters and drive by as well. That goes on for one hour. One hour is 3,600 seconds. Divided by 1.8, that equals 2,000.

So far so good. Now let's assume these cars don't drive at 100 km/h but at 50 km/h. According to our rule, the minimum distance goes down to 25 meters. The cars are closer to each other, but, because the speed is slower, it still takes an hour for 2,000 cars to pass by where you're standing. The same goes for cars at 200 km/h and 80 km/h. In fact, it's the same for every speed you pick.

So we can postulate that the maximum capacity of one lane is 2,000 cars per hour, according to this basic rule. That means the maximum capacity per lane is 48,000 cars in 24 hours. And that leads to the conclusion that a road like the A3 in Germany, near Frankfurt, with three lanes in each direction, has a maximum capacity of 144,000 cars a day in each direction.

However, if you consult the internet and look for the number of cars passing through the A3 south of Frankfurt everyday, they'll tell you that 148,000 cars pass in both directions on this road, which is 74,000 cars in each direction. This seems doable, since the road has a maximum capacity of 288,000 cars, as per our earlier calculations.

But bear in mind that these cars are not evenly spread out across the day. There are almost empty streets during the night, so those big numbers are reached during the rush hours in daytime.

If you put that all together, then you understand that traffic jams during rush hour mostly happen simply because too many people stick to the distance rule. The only way of getting enough cars through during rush hour would be with additional lanes or less distance. Not a pleasant discovery for those drivers who love safety and rules, is it? Nor for the government which refuses to change the situation and keeps giving drivers tickets for something that is not under their control.

But our subconscious mind is much cleverer than we believe. It certainly recognizes the stupidity of adhering to rules that make no sense. Without access to our subconscious mind, we do not change. So what can our mind do but give up?

If you follow all rules without careful consideration, you end up drilling stupidity into your brain. This means that you need to reconsider rules and you need to be aware of what you do. Maybe you also need to make the conscious decision to put one or the other rule aside just to see how it feels and to realise that it gives you freedom and enhances creativity. Or you can just keep conforming, as you did before.

"Life is like music, it must be composed by ear, feeling and instinct, not by rule."—Samuel Butler.

This applies to every rule that we have.

Rules are created for human beings and not the other way around.

The fifth and biggest reason why people avoid change is the thinking that the world is getting worse and all our soft approaches are not working. In order to be successful, people think that you need to be stronger and tougher than the rest. You cannot trust others, since the human being is always driven by fear, greed and laziness. Making use of these negative characteristics is the only possible way to motivate the human being.

Look at this world, they say. Everyone is working against each other and separation from other cultures seems more widespread than the creation of a global village of mutual respect and kindness.

Well, that's how it can feel when digesting what mainstream media tells us. Often, the response of an individual to ideas of "connectedness" is driven by such patterns of thought. Will we remain in that situation? Are we actually in that situation at all?

Here comes the answer to the initial question. How

come the butterfly emerges from the caterpillar? I once heard someone say that it is because the butterfly just wants to fly so much. To me, that's a rather cute motivation-oriented explanation. But I find it very interesting that there is a scientific reason available as well.

Have you ever heard of imago cells? Within the body of a caterpillar, there are imago cells. Those are special cells initiating the transformation of the caterpillar into the butterfly. Now, if an imago cell starts working, the defensive cells of the caterpillar recognize it as an enemy cell and start fighting against it. They would win against a single imago cell. But the reason why those imago cells win the battle at the end is because of their sheer number and because of the fact that they connect with each other to become bigger and bigger as a group. Because of that, the defensive system fighting passionately against the transformation loses in the long run.

Think of the world as a caterpillar, ready to transform. Everywhere, we have imago cells popping up as drivers of change in order to create a better future. Let's get together and recognise that we are working with subjects to love and not with objects to perform. The defensive system of the caterpillar is the establishment in our world; these are people who don't want to change and think everything should be left as it is. If the people who want to bring about change connect and become active, this transformation is going to work.

If I feel sad about what's happening in the world,

then I remind myself that I'm like an imago cell. It's natural that change should be fought by the old defensive systems. But if enough of the imago-cell-like individuals and organizations get active and aware of each other, then we can turn this world into a butterfly. For that, we need to stand up.

Some years ago, we did a really nice event with about 600 participants. It was an amazing experience and full of energy. I thought it was perfect. However, when the show was over, a young lady approached me backstage. I saw in her eyes that she had some feedback for me. She started by confirming how great the last 45 minutes had been for her. But then, she asked why I didn't make her stand up when we did the solo piece with the two groups giving applause to each other. Making music at that level of energy while being seated felt awkward to her.

I was about to justify myself and explain why I don't urge people to stand up. I wanted to tell her that, with her feedback in mind, I would think about altering my speech and tell people that if they want, they can stand up while they play and give applause.

But suddenly, I felt this light shining in my brain. So I said to her, "You know, I never explicitly prohibited standing up. If you had the impulse to stand up, then why did you not do it? Did you need my permission first?"

She looked at me and understood that the decision for her to stand up was with her. That's what it's all about.

Let's stick with the idea of music for a second. Have

you ever had that feeling at the end of a live concert when you want to stand up and give a standing ovation? But usually, you end up looking around the room to see if anyone else is standing up as well. Maybe the performance didn't feel perfect to everyone. How embarrassing it would be if you were the only one to stand up! This is a small example but it shows how people have a tendency to assess their personal opinions in light of mainstream reactions before having the guts to expose themselves.

Let me be precise on that one. I'm not talking about a situation (concert or real-life) where the result is crystal-clear, top-notch, first-class and obviously the best. Everyone applauds that. I'm also not talking about performances or situations which were really bad and required serious improvement. Such situations require empathy and respect, mixed with honesty.

The world can change in the grey area in-between—in situations that are uncertain and diverse. If you stand up in a concert at such a moment, you will see that many people will soon follow because they have been waiting for a pioneer like you to make a statement. Maybe half the room will stand up after a minute, just because you started the trend. And imagine what impact that can have on the future of that band.

To me, this is one of the strongest metaphors for real life.

If you have the slightest drive to stand up for something, then just f... do it. Because we need pioneers—people with courage who can become ambassadors for a better world. I'm talking about a world where globalization is interpreted and executed as a chance to make us all more connected by heart, not by business and technology.

Chapter 12 (B)
A Connection Ambassador

Chapter 10, "Connect Yourself," said it was getting personal. Well, this last chapter is very personal to me. Over three months have passed since I last worked on this book.

The whole idea of the book is to get an understanding of the huge difference between your spontaneous desires and what you require, as a human being, to live a complete and prosperous life. What's the difference between what you want and what you need?

When I look back at my last three decades, I see the gift that I've been given. I dropped music for a business career and then turned back to music to help so many other business people make music with me. Why did this make so many people and myself so happy throughout the years?

It is a paradox that, while I was writing *The Connection Phenomenon* next to running all our Drum Cafe events and trainings, I started feeling the effects of disconnectedness again. Writing a book is not an easy task, I realised. I wanted to finish the book. Five years of thinking about it had to come to fruition. But my work was no less demanding than before. And, on top of it, I had a second huge project to finish—the release of my first music album with the band that I have been playing with for over ten years. Consequently, I had to make a couple of tough decisions and set priorities.

I set aside my work and dropped an unhealthy number of routines that had great meaning to me—sports, contemplative practice, a number of Drum Cafe events that I personally facilitate, time with my wife, my family and friends, travel, relaxation, spontaneous conversations etc. Some may call this focusing on the book. In hindsight, it felt like blindness and some kind of obsession.

Additionally, this was my first book and my initial idea was to use it to support my business. This is not an unusual thing to say. People write books to sell them or to create leads. But maybe it's unusual to say this from within the book itself. Not only did I want to make it *my* personal book but I also wanted to make it a reference for all the services my business offered.

Do you understand the conflict? It was about my performance and how much the book could achieve. And I didn't even realise how distant that approach was from the original intention of the book, which was about understanding music as a tool for fostering human connectedness.

When I finished chapter 11, I was as disconnected as possible with the key elements of my life.

The question on the table was: how could I do what I *need* to do and stop chasing what I *want* to do in order to talk congruently about becoming a connection ambassador?

About 30 years ago, during my studies at the University of Applied Sciences, one major subject was control engineering. The professor was a strange character and literally all students hated him, including me. I remember his first lecture, when he opened the board and showed us a huge string of math. He explained that this was the math behind the control unit of the barrel of a Leopard II tank which became famous, since it was able to stay on target better than any other tank being driven at full speed. He said we would be able to do that math ourselves when he was finished with us. And that was the level of his lectures.

He was a nerd. And there was no way to get around him and his classes. As a result, I learned a lot about control circles and impulse responses of complex systems. This refers to how a system of any kind reacts to major change from outside.

These lessons came back to my mind recently and I understood that, behind what he'd taught me was the answer to my question.

Control engineering is a constant process of doing and sensing, adjusting and sensing again, adjusting and sensing again, and so on. That's the nature of it, and it appears to be the nature of a conscious living being as well.

When I was in performance mode, I was doing things and adjusting but not sensing. I had to set my business development ambitions and all further writing on complete hold in order to sense myself. How do I feel? How connected am I? It finally worked out only when my wife and I came to a "real" stop.

What does "real" mean in this context? There's a gap between intending to do something differently and actually doing it differently. It's not really extraordinary to use new tools and new ideas in areas where the impact is not fundamental or even existential. Hence, we pretend to change but only in areas where we control the change. That is not a big change.

Big change happens when you give up control. Raising kids, for example, has a lot to do with trust. But real trust starts only when things are unsure. And, at that time, you need great courage to remain trustful. There are moments when your whole body tells you to exercise control. Showing trust is not a big deal when a relatively harmless situation has been overdramatized by fearful fantasies and projections.

Real trust becomes an issue only in situations which present a challenge. Real love can only be experienced when real fear overcomes you. And you can only come to a complete stop when everything else in your life seems to be demanding that you act.

I came to a complete stop only when we left for a long retreat at a very busy time while the company was simultaneously hit by illness, attrition, holidays and projects. It felt like the worst possible thing to do and yet, it was what I needed. We travelled far away from all normal duties which enabled me to reconsider things completely. Finally, I found myself willing to challenge my ego trip.

In the last few weeks and months, I redistributed some of my work to a reorganized and smaller team. I focused on our core competencies and got our key contributors even closer to the heart of the company. This led to replacing all our IT with a simple but effective cloud-based software and to having agile systems in place that met our flexible working style. It led me to following a plan that my key employees came up with—implementing a focused, 30-hour workweek in the back office. It led me to closing down andante communications ltd., our consulting firm that was founded just a few years ago, in 2014, and merging the services back into Drum Cafe, now called Drum Cafe Academy, making it one integrated service from one entity with one connected brand.

These were all radical changes to set the framework for my business and I knew they would help me in the future. They were all dedicated towards making my company better rather than bigger. They led me into understanding my typical male performance conditioning and how I had the chance to change that into a healthy way of life.

When all that was done, I felt the need to revisit and revise all the chapters and write this conclusion.

A connection ambassador is someone who is able to connect all four elements of being simultaneously. That means, a connection ambassador embodies love *and* presence in the outer *and* inner world.

And he's able to teach others to do so as well.

Love is the primary level of being. Whatever you do, do it with love. Or don't do it at all. The only thing that can hold you back is fear. Fear is the opposite of love. Not hate. Hate is just another instance of love. To overcome fear, love needs to be put in place. This is because love and fear are like light and darkness, as Osho once put it. There is nothing you can do about the darkness, which is simply the absence of light. You cannot put darkness away. You can only add light in order to eliminate darkness. Switch on the light by introducing love to the scene.

You become present in the moment when you move your consciousness from focus to widespread openness at will, as and when appropriate. Everything that has the strength to make you present in the moment should be part of your daily routine so that it becomes part of your way of life over time.

Lastly, you need to understand both, the outer and the inner world as two sides of life with almost antithetical rules.

The material world that drives so much of our way of life is full of limited resources: material things, time, possessions, money and physical energy. At this side of the world, the basic principle is that if you give things away for free, you have less than before for yourself. If you give money to a stranger in need, this means you will have less money in your own pocket. Your outer world shrinks.

It is a misunderstanding to think that being nice in the material world will serve you well and give you more in return, on a material level. It is a business world where you basically invest more to gain more. It correlates with what I say in chapter 3, "Business Connections." You can achieve a great deal by being agile, enthusiastic and cooperative. It is important to succeed in this world and accept its rules and dynamics because this is the world that you're supposed to live in.

At the same time, the inner world is the complete opposite. Here, you have unlimited resources: presence and love, fantasy, positive thoughts and spiritual energy. At this side of the world, the basic principle is unlimited and free giving which results in getting much more in return, for yourself. You can spend unconditionally here, and it always comes back to you twofold.

This correlates with chapter 4, "Inner Connections," where you develop inner peace, inner joy and love for what you do and how you are. If you give money to a stranger for free, then you're giving away a limited resource in the outer world. But you can also decide to give it together with your unconditional love from your inner world. Don't expect any payback in the outer world. It will come to your inner world. And that is what finally matters. You can grow in your inner world, which will help you understand your purpose in the outer world.

If you focus on the outer world only, it might become full of material things, but it might feel empty and it may not matter much to you or anybody else on a deeper level. On the other hand, exclusively seeking all answers from the mystics or a higher, inner being will cut you off from real living. If you do this, you might end up looking down on the secular, commercial world and become what I like to call spiritually arrogant.

Understanding and mastering the dynamics of both, the inner and outer worlds, and practicing two ways of being i.e., presence (originally male) and love (originally female), in both worlds will make your own life and the life of others more meaningful. Doing this will make you into a connection ambassador.

Mahatma Gandhi said, "The best way to find yourself is to lose yourself in the service of others."

I think that what he meant is: do what you must to support yourself (inner world) but do it for others (outer world). That makes a lot of sense because it will help you to stick with it. That's what made it easy for me.

Making music together with other people has all those dimensions and that's what provides a healing effect and a point of reference to those who attend. No one needs to be an expert in music in order to feel and use its connecting effects. To make music, the musician inside of you needs music theory as much as a bird needs ornithology to fly.

Every day gives you one more chance to change. I invite you to have your first day as a connection ambassador, in fact, why don't you start tomorrow?

The first thing you should do in the morning is decide what you want to be. There is an ancient Indian creation story that I consider helpful in making that decision.

After God created the world, he began to develop living beings. First, he created the shell. The shell had a rather boring life. She filtered water all day long. She just had to open and shut her mouth throughout the day.

Then God created the eagle. God gave the eagle long wings and, along with these, came the freedom to fly over mountains, seas and valleys. But God also gave the eagle the responsibility of feeding and raising its offspring.

Then God created man. First he brought him to the shell which was opening and shutting her mouth and then to the eagle, which floated freely over the cliffs and had to chase food. And man had to decide which of these lives he wanted to live.

In fact, we still face the same big decision everyday: do we want the life of the shell or do we want the life of the eagle? Whatever your choice for the day is, be present in that role and don't waste your time regretting. You always have the chance to make a new choice tomorrow. The days when you can act as a connection ambassador are the days of the eagle.

When you have your first conversation of the day or run your first meeting in the office, take the lead and remember to synchronize the people first. Feed them with connectedness like the eagle feeds its young ones with food.

The method that has become a key experience for me is a humming exercise. It is very simple and I do it with my musicians every time I go on stage. The more stressed out we are prior to the event, the more I make it a priority to do this properly.

We form a circle and put our arms around our neighbours. We close our eyes, take a deep breath and simultaneously hum a tone. The goal is not to have the longest hum or the highest or lowest tone. The goal is to synchronize our breath to start and stop together and to let the humming flow to form a unique harmony for that day.

No harmony or disharmony is right or wrong. It just is what it is. We do it a minimum of three times. After that, we open our eyes in a receptive mode, not longing for something with our eyes but acknowledging the team around us. Every single team member makes eye contact with every other team member. Only when that is completely finished (yes, that can take a while if the team has 10 people in it) do we start talking and open up the circle.

This is singing in a simple way and creates rapid

synchronicity in both, breathing and listening, that instantly connects the participants. The soaring sounds created will not take long to touch you deep in your heart and soul. Every group performance, be it on stage or in a meeting room, will improve massively if propelled by this start.

Today, approach your team and introduce this method. Stop rehearsing and start doing. It's like learning a language. Reading a textbook to learn a language will take a lot of time. But visit the country where that language is spoken and fall in love with a local person. Then you'll see how rapid learning works.

Similarly, just go where you want to go and fall in love with what you do and see how fast you can become an expert at it. You want to learn a contemplative practice? Don't sit in your room rehearsing. Pick one simple exercise, like the humming exercise. Learn it fairly well but show it quicker than you'd planned to other people. Tell them that you've found something new and make it a group exercise. If it flies, it flies. If not, try something else. You will get great results and you'll get them much faster than anticipated.

Make all your actions part of what I call a "Rumi field." There is one poem by the Sufi mystic, Rumi, that I especially like. This is how I would summarize it in my own words: "There is a field out there where everything just is what it is, without judgment and comparison. Nothing is wrong, nothing is right. Nothing is better than the other, nothing weaker, nothing stronger. On that field, we will meet at perfect eye level in order to play and grow together."

When you work with a team, keeping these words in mind, you will see massive potential being uncovered right in front of you.

And finally, never stop remembering tools like the barometer of connectedness, the scale of words and others which can help you to connect with yourself and (re)connect with people and everything around you. Make all your actions supportive of others.

As the Dalai Lama said, "Our prime purpose in this life is to help others. And if you can't help them, at least don't hurt them."

Outlook (C)
Fadeout: Final Words

I often get asked about my views on the future of our workplaces. To me, it is rather simple. The future of our workplaces lies in humanity. Machines can't be human. Otherwise, they wouldn't be called machines, right? Digitalization will never get to the level of analogue beings. Automation is always somewhat mechanical and what is mechanical will not please anyone.

Jobs that provide a human touch to the customer will remain. Hence the need to make human development our priority. We haven't changed that much, biologically speaking, in the last 5,000-10,000 years as mentioned earlier in this book. Our genes are pretty much the same as in those ancient days. All our development has been of the cultural and ethical sort.

But ethics is often mixed up with religion and therefore misinterpreted. And culture is the first thing we are willing to sacrifice if we have to tighten our budgets. We need each and every individual to turn that around. This is needed to form that network of imago cells willing to lead into the metamorphosis of the world from caterpillar to butterfly.

With that in mind, you may approach people you meet with your idea of how your interaction can start with a connecting exercise. Be present and make eye contact if you want to stick to the basics. A silent moment, a true hug, some serious listening, X/Y clapping, a humming exercise or even the knee La Ola can be done if you want to be progressive. Do anything of your choice that you feel comfortable with.

Smile. Look into the other person's eyes. And give it a go.

"Shall We?"

Sources and Further Information

As you can see, there is no typical 10-page list of references attached. I don't even try to reference the many scientific books that prove the effects of making music together to the individual and our society. All the information in this books originates from my experience working with many audiences as well as my thoughts and findings about that experience. Where I referenced specific sources or books for support, I did this right in the text. This book can only start you off on your journey. If you want to continue your journey using further sources, then refer to the end of chapter 7.

If you want a live experience of how your team or group can gain from the concepts outlined in this book, then please visit our worldwide services at

http://drumcafe.matthias-jackel.com

(you can switch between German and English on the page)

Testimonials

Out of the many feedbacks we get on the events and keynotes, I've selected some for the appendix to the book. I'm very thankful to these clients for allowing me to print their feedback, underlining the positive results achieved in our events, keynotes, trainings and workshops.

Matthias Jackel provided 8 keynotes to our GEDANKENtanken format in 2016 and 2017 to audiences from 500 to 2.000 people, all concerned about teamwork, communication and the togetherness between the human being. It was plain amazing to see how all those groups melted into a pod and became one just through music.

Dr. Stefan Frädrich,
Author of several famous books
VP of GEDANKENtanken
(i.e., "Revuel your thoughts"),
the German equivalent of TED Talks.

Matthias and I have been working for many years and I had him run interactive shows at several of my life coaching events to audiences from 200 to 2.000 people. What he does is as simple as it is amazing: showing the audiences how it feels to come to an unexpected achievement together as a group. A perfect match to one of the core messages of my events that we as a person can achieve far more than we believe if we just do it and get the support of our people around.

Christian Bischoff,
Top German Personal and Life Coach and
Inventor of the Life Coaching Event
"The Art of Doing Your Thing"

It appears to me that Matthias must have the best job in the world. Wherever he shows up on stage, he creates that amazing euphoria and positive vibe in the audience, again and again and again. It's worth reading this book to understand what the source of that effect is.

Gerhard Kulhavy,
Founder and CEO of Speakers Excellence.
The number one source for top speakers
and keynotes in Germany.

Utilizing music, Matthias Jackel is creating a unique metaphor for the inseparability of human beings, thus creating a basis for team play and individual prosperity.

Michael Reinhold,
Musicworx
Known from Dragon's Den Germany

I was one of the participants of that fantastic workshop with E.ON in Copenhagen. I´m in HR and have been in the field for almost 20 years. I´ve designed and participated in a number of leadership trainings, workshops etc. over the years, and there comes a time when events start to look a lot like each other; there might even be a tendency towards becoming blasé... And then someone comes along and changes the scenery altogether!

The workshop you did with us stuck with me and all my colleagues better than any presentation made during the two days spent at Kastrup. You delivered such a clear and sincere message, so honestly value-based and so perfectly illustrated by the music, it created a short circuit straight to the heart and mind. And that´s where it lingers. I´m truly amazed by the strong impact of the workshop and was so filled with energy and decisiveness (still am) afterwards.

Yesterday, we had a different workshop, with a large number of managers. One part of it was a visit by a team that had just won one of our biggest deals ever. Before they came in, our CEO said, "Let´s do what we did in Copenhagen. Let´s make their eyes sparkle." And they entered the room to huge applause and cheering that filled the room. Lots of sparkling eyes there!

So this is my feedback and I would like to thank you for one of the best workshops I´ve ever participated in.

Thank you so much and I wish you all the best.

Jennie Kullberg
HR Business Partner E.ON

Acknowledgements

All my thanks go to the people and resources who've helped me writing this book.

To *Sabine Vieten*, my key Drum Cafe facilitator on stage and most important business partner, who I have the honour to work and grow with together. Not only did Sabine review my book, she's an amazing inspiration and a female enabler to so many processes. Thanks for your trust, ideas and commitment. You are a connection ambassador!

Many thanks to the whole *Drum Cafe Germany team* in the back office and on stage, people who make our services come true to our audiences and who not only deliver excellent work (special thanks go to *Jenni Dietrich* here, who always kept things moving in the office while I was 'somewhere' writing on this book) but also show the level of extraordinary connectedness that is so important in our doing.

Also, great thanks to *Brett Schlesinger* and *Warren Lieberman* for starting this partnership with me almost 15 years ago. It is not easy to distinguish between business and private relationship since friendship and working together with all of you just merged into something bigger.

There have been many individuals as well in helping the book look like it is. *Tetsuro Chirahada* who made that great cover photo while I was over to Japan to support the Nico Nico Smile project, right after the disaster of the earthquake and Tsunami.

Mario Andreya for my portrait on the back cover, who made all the great portraits of the Drum Cafe Germany team over the course of the last years. Thomas Satori who created the graphics in the book.

Natasa Denman, Stuart Denman and *Moustafa Hamwi* for leading me through this process and making the book come true. A special thanks go to all the other many people and companies that I had the honour to meet and work with that influenced my life and my thinking. A thousand thanks to all of you.

My final words and biggest thanks go to my wife *Alexandra 'Akeesha' Jackel*. Worth a chapter on its own. For all the years Alexandra supported me in the idea of writing this book and further developing the concepts that emerged from running the Drum Cafe events. Endless conversations and reviews happened about the content and life in general and it was her who remained positive and connected with me when I was focussing on content delivery so much that I struggled to remain connected with myself and anything around me. You always extended and keep extending my views. With you, I feel home.

The special characters in the content page (music notes) are available for free download at www.dafont.com and named "Lassus" by David Rakowski.

Drum Cafe Logo and the name Drum Cafe are trademarks owned by Drum Cafe SA.

The life-graph picture in chapter "Connect Yourself" is made and owned by Matthias Jackel.

www.ingramcontent.com/pod-product-compliance
Lightning Source LLC
Chambersburg PA
CBHW071910290426
44110CB00013B/1343